A Guide to Getting It:

Achieving Abundance

E. Thomas Costello • Marilyn French Hubbard
Stephanie McDilda • Nancy Mindes
Schuyler Morgan • Cathy Nealon
Gail Ostrishko • Marilyn Schwader
Jordana Tiger • Claire Walsh

Foreword by Bijan Anjomi

Mari

D1166860

CLARITY OF VISION PUBLISHING • PORTLAND, OREGON

For more information, visit www.ClarityOfVision.com
To order a book, visit www.AGuideToGettingIt.com

Book Design and Production by Marilyn Schwader

ISBN 0-9716712-1-4
Library of Congress Control Number: 2002092863
First edition: July 2002

Table of Contents

A Note from the Editor

Everyone has the power within to achieve a life of abundance. But what is it that makes a life of prosperity seem so simple for some, and such a struggle for others? What is true abundance, after all? This is a book about discovering the power to create a life of your choice—to have what you really want, not just what you are given. Ten Life and Business Coaches have distilled their coaching methods for creating abundance down to the most important aspects to consider. *A Guide to Getting It: Achieving Abundance* contains ten chapters that offer each coach's unique perspective on how to learn the secrets of prosperity, to find abundant inner resources, and to create a life of choice.

This 160-page book is the second book in a series of books written by Life and Business Coaches that offer invaluable insights, examples, and exercises as guides to help the reader improve their business and personal life. In addition to tips and explanations, there are chapters with personal stories of how the authors or their clients faced obstacles and tragedy to discover a new view of abundance in their lives.

I invite you to read, explore, and enjoy!

Marilyn Schwader, Editor

Acknowledgements

My life is blessed with abundance, and I am grateful for the friends, family, and colleagues in my life who have helped me see and believe in that feeling of prosperity. I am especially proud to have worked with such a wonderful gathering of coaches. I am very thankful for the opportunity to read and share your thoughts, experiences, and the refreshing way you all view the world.

Marilyn Schwader, Editor

Foreword

by Bijan Anjomi

Many people believe that having prosperity and abundance means having a lot of money in the bank or owning a big house or a large company. What they don't realize, often when it is too late, is that all the money in the world does not help them if they don't have good health and wonderful relationships in their lives. Once you are in touch with that truth, your perceptions and goals will change, and you will see prosperity in its totalities. You will have peace and balance, and ultimately, complete joy.

You might say, "this is easier said than done." If you only see it in the context of following the mass consciousness of this planet, then that might be true. However, if you are willing to see it from a different point of view, then you can examine your thoughts and actions in each moment to align with what you desire. By purchasing this powerful book, you have taken the first step to seeing that new point of view—and starting on your path to abundance.

As you begin to change your view, remember that you are always the cause of whatever happens in your life. Nothing—and I mean no thing—ever comes to you without you inviting or allowing it to be in your life. You do that with your belief system, the way you think about things and yourself. Most people think life is hard, that it's a struggle, with suffering and sacrifice along the way. And that might be the way it is for them. Yet I tell you, my brothers and sisters, I know beyond the shadow of doubt that life is all joy, with exciting moments along the way. For me, life truly is that way every moment. For those who don't have the life they want, it is because of what they believe. Their way is not the "wrong" way, nor is mine the "right" way. Having our own belief system is the way each of us experiences life, good or bad.

The question is which path you have chosen for yourself in the past, and what path do you choose now? The desire to have abundance in your life is very powerful. Beginning your path to abundance, and understanding how your beliefs shape the world around you starts by picking up and reading the book that calls to you. With the ideas and tools this book provides, I believe that you are starting on that path. Learn, grow, believe, and my deepest wish— that you and everyone will have a life of total effortless prosperity— will come to you. Love and light, Bijan

Bijan Anjomi

Bijan Anjomi is the author of the book, *Absolutely Effortless Prosperity*. Through speaking engagements, television, radio, personal coaching, and his website, Bijan assists people in opening their hearts to joy and peace—experiencing it, believing in it, and living in the reality of it. He explains his vision for world peace in these simple words:

"As more and more people begin to experience joyful, peaceful, abundant living, the barriers between countries, cultures and religious philosophies will simply melt away."

Visit www.effortlessprosperity.com for more information.

A Tale of Abundance

By Marilyn Schwader

REALITY AND YOUR STORY ARE NEVER THE SAME—
REALITY IS ALWAYS KINDER. ~ BYRON KATIE

Once upon a time, there lived a young child who had a brilliant smile, a warm heart, and a sharp wit. She radiated love, and the people and events in her life returned that love in measure. Some said she was charmed, and with that belief, she felt that all of her dreams would one day come true. And so she dreamed magnificent dreams and set out to accomplish them with certainty and optimism.

At times, she would come to an obstacle on her way to accomplishing her dreams. But with her seemingly inherent knowledge of her abilities and the realization that she had the love and support of those around her, she felt that her possibilities were unlimited. She somehow sensed deep inside, that she would be able to make the right choice when she needed to and that even with the possibility of making a mistake, she would be able to pick herself back up and move on.

As her successes grew, she began to see that her perspective was different than others. She would look at a problem and see dozens of possible solutions. Others would see only the problem. They would laugh about her optimism and her ability to see the silver lining in the clouds. And they would shake their heads and say, "Someday she'll realize that dreams are just that—dreams. She really should learn how to be realistic."

As she left the support and outlook of her childhood friends and family to travel her path, and grew into a young woman, the voices of optimism grew less abundant and other voices crowded into her head. The voices were limiting and fearful. "Don't dream big. You'll only be disappointed." "You can't do that, it's just not within your capabilities." "Nobody has ever done that before. What makes you think you can?" The voices grew louder. Despite her resiliency and her open heart, they started to affect her. Those voices came from people who were older and had seen more of the world. She started to believe that she must conform to them. After all, if all of the voices around her were saying the same thing, doesn't that mean that they must be right?

And so, she began to question her beliefs, and wonder about her dreams. She stopped listening to her heart and her head took over. If the choice was not logical, she wouldn't do it. If someone told her she wasn't being realistic, she would change directions. Her head took the lead, and in a short time, she stopped dreaming. Dreams were unrealistic, and that meant she would never be able to accomplish them. Why even allow herself to hope? Just stay the course. Don't look at other possibilities. Remain safe, because that's what's expected.

And soon, the light inside of her died. She grew dark and full of fear. And in a very short time, others who were dark and full of fear surrounded her. They filled her mind with truisms and limited beliefs. They squelched her creativity and trounced on her hope. And every decision became a struggle, because she couldn't find it in her heart to see the truth. She began to make up stories about why she couldn't succeed. The judgements she made of herself and others came next, and the lies followed in a short time. She stopped trusting herself, and soon she stopped trusting others, too. In a short time she was in a spiral, a downward cycle into a chasm of disbelief and despair. She struggled with her self-esteem, her relationships, and ultimately with her purpose in life.

Somewhere deep inside of her, she knew that this wasn't the way to be. But, in the struggle to survive amidst the negative energy swirling within and around her, she couldn't seem to find the answer or the energy to change. Doing anything different would require enormous courage, and that had left her long ago. The only thing she could see was how difficult change would be. Even though she was miserable, at least she knew where she was. That horizon out there had become too distant. She might get there and drop off the edge. Why even make an effort?

And so she drifted along in life. At times she felt inklings about what she might do differently. And those feelings, they seemed so real. But they were only echoes of her dreams, of her heart telling her to listen to the whispers. She had long ago built layers within her to block out any possibility of having to feel. Allowing herself to listen to that ancient wisdom of intuition would certainly make her look foolish. She couldn't put herself in that light. What would others think? That would reveal her vulnerability.

Her inklings grew and so did her concern about how she had gotten off track. But she didn't believe she had the time or energy to do anything about it. Things around her were crumbling, and she desperately struggled to put out the fires, to handle the crises. And her fear grew. Where she had once imagined unlimited possibilities, they now seemed non-existent. She could only maintain. To extinguish the pain, she began to medicate herself with one addiction after another. Although they blocked out her thoughts, the pain remained. Her heart still hurt. So she wrapped herself in a cocoon of misery and shut herself off from all the people in her life who might have helped her. Her feeling of lack was in full bloom. Crisis had become a way of life.

One day, she thought she heard a voice. The source seemed so distant. Yet, it was familiar. At first, she thought it was inside her head, for she knew it hadn't come from outside of her. She became still and listened again. No, it wasn't a voice; it was a feeling, a trembling. And it was coming from that place buried years ago—her heart. "That can't be," she thought. "I haven't felt anything for so long, how could anything still exist there?" And so she suppressed it once again. Too scary; too much to think about.

And so, the universal source from which all things flow, which had provided her with so many opportunities to change, sent her one last message.

She awoke with a start, her fingers grasping at the steering wheel as the truck she was driving veered into the median. She pulled hard to the right and back onto the road. The truck pitched to that direction. Too much. She swung the steering wheel back to the left and the truck followed her lead. And then, it took over from the momentum of the 85-mile per hour speed. She felt the right, rear of the truck begin to pull down as the front left started to rise. The vehicle rolled once, then twice. Then she lost count. The inside of the cab became a chamber of horrors as the rolling continued. She held her arms above her head, as if she could keep the crushing blows of the rolling vehicle from crashing down around her.

No time to pray, no time to right all that had been in her life, all that had led her to this point. No time to say, "I'm sorry," or "Why wasn't I more grateful?" Only time to feel the wrath of uncontrollable movement, of thousands of pounds of machine rolling her like a doll until the churning finally came to a stop. And then, for a brief moment, there was a jarring silence. Where but a moment before she faced as sure a death as she had ever feared, she had been spared.

With her vehicle on its side and she dangling in her seatbelt, the full realization of what had happened slowly began to seep into the deeply bruised cells of her brain. For the first time in her life, there had been utter, total, incredible chaos. She had no control. Her world had not just been turned upside down; it had been thrown about like feathers in the wind, only to settle across a swath of a 100 yards or so along the ditch of an interstate highway.

She and her passenger were alive. Of that, she was almost certain. But how could they be? No one should have survived that kind of turbulence. All she could think about was the tremendous amount of damage and loss she had caused.

And yet, there was no blood. Her passenger was talking and moving. Not even a broken bone for either of them.

She found the seat belt release and clicked the button. The truck had landed with the passenger side down. She looked up at the driver's side window and realized that the glass was gone. Standing up in the heavily damaged cab, their heads popped through the window. They pulled themselves up and out of the wreckage and surveyed the carnage around them.

Her life was unalterably changed in those moments. Although the shock and severe concussion fogged her brain for weeks, she gradually began to see that the accident had, in an ironic twist, saved her life. The universe had created the chaos—the disorderly mass that precedes the existence of order—to wake her up. Nearly at the bottom of an abyss of self-doubt, fear, and hopelessness, the universe had shaken, but not destroyed her. It had given her an opportunity to climb out of the hole she had been digging for herself, to choose to live life to its fullest, and to accomplish all of those dreams she had pushed aside for years.

She began her journey back to abundance by writing down a list of all of the things that she had wanted to do since she was a child. To learn to dance the salsa and rumba, raft the Grand Canyon, take voice lessons, plant a garden, enjoy friends, gather with family, to write a book, travel to distant lands. To live life with joy and gratitude, to take risks, to live from a place of love, not fear. She saw that fear had been sucking the life from her, and life was already too short to have a leak in it like that. The accident had shown her how life could end in an instant. She determined that she would embrace each remaining moment.

She began to see that the story she believed about her life was just that: her story. The truth was that she had the choice to follow someone else's reality, or to create her own. All those voices saying that she must be realistic were seeing their own reality, not hers. They didn't believe she could accomplish her dreams, because they hadn't accomplished their own. Their view of her capabilities was really them looking at their own, and not believing in them.

She looked up the definition of reality. It read: "Reality is something that constitutes a real or actual thing, as distinguished from something that is merely apparent." And she saw that her dreams could be big—and realistic, because they were her truth, her reality.

She realized that parts of her story pointed a finger at others, placing responsibility on them, and making her the victim. She now saw that throughout all of the good and the bad that had happened to her, she was the only common denominator, the only constant. She was the one who had made the choices and decisions that created the situations and the story lines. Oh, how easy it seemed to blame others for where she was in her life. And how dearly she had paid for not taking responsibility for her own choices.

Looking at the people in her life, she saw that most of them were not friends, but acquaintances. They would gladly take from her, but weren't willing to give back when she had a need for their support. They liked her for whom she was, but became envious when she outshone them. She started to surround herself with people who were growing and dreaming, and who believed in their abilities, and in hers. She eliminated lack thinkers and energy vampires from her world, and began to seek doers and optimists, for they expanded her view and lifted her mind. She found ordinary people who were accomplishing extraordinary things. And her belief in her own ability to achieve soared.

She looked at her possessions, and saw that her life was cluttered with things that didn't fill her anymore. She packed boxes of clothes and belongings and gave them away. What others might not use, she tossed in the trash. Clearing her space created a vacuum into which even more riches and energy flowed. When guests visited, they commented on how open her house seemed and how nice they felt when they walked into a room. Her energy expanded, even with seemingly less in her life.

Seeing the reward of giving, and knowing how much she had to share, she volunteered to help others. Providing time and money to benefit the less fortunate expanded her heart even more. Her life was blessed. She saw how much she could offer to those who hadn't yet found their abundance.

She started to write down all that she had in her life, and even more appeared. She began to see more clearly how much she had worried about the past and those things she couldn't change, and about the future and what she couldn't control. Living each moment as it happened, being present and whole, she began to feel again, and like the petals of a flower in spring, her emotional wisdom blossomed. Crying and laughter became spontaneous; envy and anger dissolved. Her mind was free of expectations and interpretations, and her spirit soared.

As she sought new people, new beliefs, and new experiences, she soon began attracting good things in her life. The more she responded with love from within, the more the universe began to shower her with love in return. And soon, with gratitude, love, and joy emanating from her heart again, her life was filled with abundance. Abundance, not in what she could buy, but in the simple pleasures of the day. The abundance of a child's radiance, of a beautiful painting, the unconditional love of a pet, the glory of a heartfelt laugh, the absolute joy in touching nature, the simple strains of a peaceful melody and the beating rhythm of a symphony, the exhilaration of a friend's hug, and the sensuous touch of a lover's hand. Bills became blessings, because they had provided her with the wonders of electricity, the telephone, heat, and things that made her life easier and more enjoyable. She had always had everything she needed. But now she understood just how much was in her life, and how grateful she was for it all.

Now, people notice the sparkle in her eye, the light that has returned. They see the glow and confidence grow. When she enters a room, she feels the energy of her childhood, the brilliance and certainty. With gratitude for everyday joys and humbleness for her opportunity to experience all that life has to offer, she is thankful to the power within and around her for helping her see the path of love once more. Where there was once dust and barrenness in her view, there are now multiple layers of color. There is acceptance, openness, and choice, in all of the colors of the rainbow.

She now recognizes when her heart is missing from the story. She sees when the voices don't match hers, and her values aren't in alignment with other people's views. When there is struggle, she goes to the quiet place within and feels the answer. She looks within and around herself at what makes her life abundant and full, what gives her life purpose and meaning. Throughout all that has been, and all that has brought her to this point, she now knows that her source of abundance—her purpose in life—is to be truthful and clear in her storytelling.

And if she can make even one life breathe easier by telling her tale, she will live happily ever after…

About
Marilyn Schwader

As a Writing and Life Coach, Marilyn uses humor, compassion, and a strong sense of a writer's abilities to support and motivate her clients to become published authors. She has found that her purpose in life is to give a voice to subjects that benefit others. Her mission is to provide truthful, clear, and motivating information to those who passionately desire more in their lives. Her vision is to use her two passions—coaching and storytelling—to convey this information to as many people as possible.

Marilyn graduated from Oregon State University in Corvallis, Oregon with a Bachelor of Science degree in Technical Journalism with emphasis in Business Management. After working for several years as a technical writer contracting to high tech companies in the United States and Pacific Rim countries, she veered from the writing path and started her first business, M's Tea & Coffee House, in Corvallis.

Five years and numerous disastrous business mistakes later, she left the restaurant business and a short time later discovered Coaching. In 1998 she enrolled in Coach University and started Clarity of Vision, a Business and Life Coaching practice. The law of attraction soon worked its magic, and her talents and experience in writing soon began drawing writing clients to her business.

During this time, Marilyn undertook a three-year project to compile and publish a book about her mother's family history. From that experience, she began helping people self-publish their books. Looking for a way to combine her coaching and writing experience, Marilyn decided to create a book series that would be written by coaches and that highlighted principles and ideas supported in the coaching process.

Thus, the *A Guide to Getting It* book series was born. *A Guide to Getting It: Self-Esteem* was published in January 2002. *A Guide to Getting It: Achieving Abundance* is the second in the series. Two more books are slated for publication in 2002: *A Guide to Getting It: Remarkable Management Skills* and *A Guide to Getting It: A Clear, Compelling Vision*.

For more information about Clarity of Vision Publishing, visit www.ClarityOfVision.com. To find out more about the *A Guide to Getting It* book series, visit www.AGuideToGettingIt.com. To contact Marilyn, send an email to Marilyn@ClarityOfVision.com or call 503-460-0014.

Defining Abundance

By Gail Ostrishko

Achieving abundance requires first that we define it...Define abundance?

- Is abundance having everything you wanted? Every thing you need?
- Is it a destination...a place, an experience, a state of being?
- Is it a feeling...a sense of accomplishment or satisfaction?
- How do you recognize abundance in your life?
- How do others recognize your abundance?
- What are the ultimate risks and rewards for seeking abundance in our lives?

Abundance, like beauty, is in the eye of the beholder. This is why many people simply overlook the abundance in their lives. They are basing their idea of abundance on someone else's definition, rather than their own. There are many views of abundance—monetary wealth and prosperity, physical possessions, professional accomplishments, loving relationships, spiritual serenity, and for some, the enjoyment of a simple life. For many, the external world of media, greed, and competition defines their sense of abundance. Yet even when they reach these "worldly" goals, something is often missing.

Abundance is more of an attitude than an achievement. Who you are and how you live is more of what abundance is about than what you have or where you are in life. Abundance is a sense of having more than you need. It is not about having everything you want, but flows from wanting what you have...knowing in your head and your heart that you are blessed and worthy.

The word abundance is derived from the Latin *abundare*, meaning to overflow. Its original meaning referred to the ability to recognize, appreciate, and celebrate life. Webster's definition of abundance is plentiful, rich, and full to overflowing.

Abundance is a connection with spirit revealed through living true to our hearts. We are spiritual beings living a human experience. That is why we call ourselves human beings, not human doings.

In this chapter, I offer you a conceptual framework for understanding universal aspects of human behavior, along with avenues for pursuing abundance. Personal examples, thought-provoking questions, scripture, and quotes expand application opportunities. The combination is designed to offer insight and awaken your intuition regarding your own definition and recognition of abundance.

Knowing What You Want and Getting What You Need!

I was drawn to write about defining abundance, given my strong belief in the universal truth that **Perception is Reality**. Things are not as they are; they are as we perceive them to be. Consider the research on eyewitnesses of automobile accidents. There are as many different accounts of the scene as there are witnesses.

I was trained years ago as a helping professional in Dr. William Glasser's work on Choice Theory and Reality Therapy. These models have been a permanent foundation in my life and apply in every arena of my profession as well. Choice Theory is an explanation of human behavior rooted in the belief that our brain is a system designed to maintain a sense of control over our lives. Reality Therapy is the application of that theory in the helping profession. We call it Total Quality Management in leadership circles, Appreciative Inquiry in organizational development, and Self Evaluation in personal application. Though it may have different names in various arenas, these sound principles provide a firm foundation for understanding and influencing behavior and relationships.

Basic Psychological Needs: Our Genetic Instructions

Given that our survival needs for food, safety, and shelter are met, we all have the same basic psychological needs for Love, Power, Fun, and Freedom. These needs are actually our genetic instructions, and guide our choices and relationships. All choices are rooted in the desire to meet one or more of these needs. Happiness, success, and a sense of abundance are by-products of leading a balanced, need-satisfied life. Understanding these needs as goals of behavior in others and ourselves provides powerful wisdom for effective living. While we all have the same basic needs, we have very different perceptions regarding how to meet those needs. Abundant living requires that we meet and balance our needs within the context of our own lives (behavior and experiences) and our relationships with others.

Love: Belonging, Connection with Others

We all need to feel a sense of love, belonging, and connection with others and ourselves. This connection comes in many forms and manifests through a variety of behaviors. Defining Love and Belonging is tricky because we all seek and express it differently. Some express love through physical affections such as hugs and kisses, while others may choose words, deeds, or gifts.

Power: Self-Esteem

Each of us needs to feel a sense of power and control over our lives, along with a strong sense of self worth. Seeking this power from within, rather than from the external world and others, is important. Self-esteem is your belief in yourself. If you think you can or you think you can't, you are right!

Fun: Relaxing and Renewing

Believe it or not, we have a genetic need for fun. Fun relates to diversion and enjoyment, relaxing and renewing. The tricky part is defining it! Why do we keep coming back to having to define everything? Because we are all different and we have our own definitions and perceptions of fun.

Freedom: Choices

Freedom comes in many forms and is subject to definition as well. Many associate freedom with physical and financial independence. I relate freedom to flexibility and choices. Choices are a huge source of freedom and, at the same time, bring with them responsibilities. Choosing to have a child or not is a good example of freedom of choice and the responsibilities that come with it.

Distinguishing Between Wants and Needs

We actually need very little to be content. The belief that we need what we want often prevents us from experiencing the abundance that is our birthright. Discernment between wants and needs is a fine art. I remember my mother reminding me of this consistently as I was growing up. I tried my best to convince her that I really NEEDED Nike's and Levi's. After all, everyone else had them, and without them, I felt like a total geek. Of course my mother, raising three children on her own, knew that I needed shoes and clothes, but assured me that Trax and Wranglers would suffice. If I wanted name brand clothes, I needed to save my own money. One of our oldest family stories is about my emotional devastation upon learning that my favorite outfit came from a discount store named King's! My appreciation for the outfit decreased dramatically when I learned it was discount rather than designer attire.

When I got to high school, it was the little yellow Sunbird I needed! It was the cutest car I had ever seen (in my price range) and it was my favorite color! Mom said no again, because it didn't have air conditioning. According to her, I needed air conditioning. I thought this was a want! Well, you know how the story goes… mother is always right! While wants tend to be tangible and materialistic, needs tend to be more intrinsic.

One of my needs is to nurture, especially children and families, which made my first "real job" as an in-home family counselor a good fit. While in the process of building our own family through open adoption, I find that volunteering as a wish grantor with the Make a Wish Foundation gives me the opportunity to nurture in a very unique and special way. I knew that the families that I touched would be grateful for my deeds, which they are. What has been more amazing is the abundance of support, generosity, and genuine desire to participate within the community. Through just one wish, many people connect and experience love, providing power to sick children and their families, while giving them the freedom to dream and do whatever their hearts desire. There is nothing more abundant than that!

I also deliver Meals on Wheels. I chose this particular opportunity in honor of my mother. Though no longer alive, I honor her presence in my life by continuing to provide an important service, which she valued and benefited from. While I really would like to have my mom back, I meet my need to nurture and connect with her generation through volunteering. Through this experience, the abundance she brought to my life lives on in spite of her passing.

The Perceptual Lens

THROUGH HIS THOUGHTS, MAN HOLDS THE KEY TO EVERY SITUATION AND CONTAINS WITHIN HIMSELF THAT TRANSFORMING AND REGENERATIVE AGENCY BY WHICH HE MAY MAKE HIMSELF WHAT HE WILLS.

~ JAMES ALLEN FROM AS A MAN THINKETH

We each view the world through our personal perceptual lens…and our perceptions create our reality. We perceive on several different levels, which ultimately combine to give meaning to our experiences. The deeper the level of perception we connect through, the stronger our connection and commitment to that perception will be.

The three levels of perception are:

- **Sensory**: information gathered through our senses.
- **Knowledge and Experience**: our personal history of experiences and knowledge.
- **Values**: the attributes and qualities we hold sacred.

Imagine your perceptual system as concentric circles within a pair of binoculars. When we look through the large end, we see a very small, distant image. This is the view when we focus our attention on the sensory level of perception. Now consider viewing through the small end of the binoculars, representing the values level of perception. The image is much larger, clearer, and magnified. Our values bring clarity and meaning to our relationships and experiences.

For example, when I was working as an in-home family counselor early in my career, I drove a Saab. Consider your knowledge and experience with Saabs. What comes to mind for most people is the significant cost of this European sports car. I suspect that my clients thought I was rich, or that I had materialistic values, both reasonable assumptions from a sensory level. The fact is that shortly after being married, my husband was driving my little Dodge Challenger at a rate of about 25 mph when a truck running a stop sign hit him. My car was totaled, and my husband could have been killed. After this experience, safety became a core value for me. So we researched automobile safety and learned that Saabs and Volvos were the safest on the road, so eventually we bought one of each! Not being aware of this experience, you might attribute different values regarding the purchase of a Saab.

Consider your lens as similar to a video surveillance camera, on duty 24/7, constantly focusing in and out, taking in and filtering information through the various levels of perception. We take in information through what we see, hear, taste, touch, and feel. Though we all may look at the same thing, the filter of our knowledge and experience gives it personal meaning. The values we embrace dictate the importance we place on the particular item or experience.

Video cameras and binoculars are available in a variety of sizes, uses, and levels of quality. This metaphor parallels the knowledge and experience aspect of our perceptions. Our filter has various options, and operates at different levels of effectiveness based on our current investment. We find that different situations and relationships call for and offer different features, and specific knowledge and experiences weigh differently in different situations.

Our perceptual lens can also be compared to a kaleidoscope. With one small shift the picture changes forever. And though we may all look through the same kaleidoscope, each of us will see something different.

Knowledge of the perceptual system provides a foundation for understanding yourself and others. Sharing and comparing our perceptions with others in order to establish shared meaning is the core of effective relationships. We often tell others their perceptions are inaccurate when they do not match our own; we suggest they "look through our lens" and adopt our reality instead. In the words of Steven Covey in his book, *The 7 Habits of Highly Effective People* we increase our effectiveness and build strong relationships when we: "Seek first to understand, then to be understood."

Our perceptions are grounded in a larger paradigm of either abundance or scarcity. The attitude of abundance is rooted in the belief that resources are abundant in the world and that all we need is available to us in infinite proportions. The scarcity mentality operates from a belief in limited resources. People who embrace this paradigm see the world through fear filters. In this mindset, the world is like a pie with a finite number of slices; if one person gets a large slice, there is less pie left for everyone else. This frame of reference breeds competition, hoarding, and difficulty sharing success, recognition, and material possessions as a result of the zero-sum mentality. Be aware of your personal paradigm, as it shapes every aspect of your life!

NOTHING IS ENOUGH TO THE MAN FOR WHOM ENOUGH IS TOO LITTLE.
~ EPICURUS

ONCE YOU LEARN THAT LESS IS MORE, ENOUGH BECOMES PLENTY
AND YOUR ENTIRE OUTLOOK ON LIFE IS TRANSFORMED.
~ UNKNOWN

Areas and Avenues of Abundance

Now that you have a model by which to view your perceptions, let's apply it to areas of abundance in your life: Spiritual, Physical, Emotional, and Financial.

Spiritual Abundance

Connection with Spirit is the cornerstone of abundance, a very powerful and personal source of internal wisdom with infinite access by everyone! Whether this means a higher power, an internal wisdom, or a broader connection with the universe, connection with spirit is paramount to the ongoing ability to recognize, embrace, and experience the infinite abundance in your life and in the world around you.

Over the past several years, I have come to understand a distinct difference between spirituality and religion. While religion breeds spirituality, inspiration means literally IN SPIRIT. Connecting with spirit evolves as we live true to our authentic selves. I have been pleasantly surprised by the connection I have made with spirit through activities as simple as walking my dog or watering flowers, to those as challenging as learning to play the guitar and attempting to adopt a baby. I had no idea how universal our connection with spirit and with one another was until I embraced this conscious journey.

- On a sensory level, many people associate spiritual abundance with organized religion. Some people have had positive experiences related to this, and others' experiences have been less desirable.
- We have varied knowledge and experience with different religions, and there are many similarities and differences among them all.
- Though various religions differ in practices and philosophies, all share the same core value regarding a greater power...a universal spiritual force that connects everything and everybody.

Physical Abundance

Physical abundance refers to physical health, having the energy and longevity to pursue what you enjoy. One without the other is useless. Maintaining our physical health is a cornerstone to enjoying abundance in all areas of life. Unfortunately, this type of abundance is one that some take for granted until it is gone. For example, consider a near death experience or terminal illness. Though I have not personally encountered either, every account I have heard of emphasizes a profound and sacred revelation of existing abundance.

If you happen to be among the 80 percent of the general population that does not exercise regularly, I respectfully suggest: JUST DO IT! Most aversion to exercise evolves from our perception of it. Evaluate your definition of exercise. As you know, perception is reality, and there are different strokes for different folks...

Explore something of interest to you. Develop some type of active hobby. Consider exercise through the perceptual lens model:

- At the sensory level, exercise can be a lot like work to many. It takes time and energy and may not generate the immediate results desired.

- On the knowledge and experience level, research has consistently confirmed the positive impact of exercise on health and longevity. Some people have negative experiences related to physical activity, often dating back to PE class! Is that what is holding you back?

- At the values level, most people value health and longevity. Thus, enduring the immediate aversion some may have to exercise will bring the long-term results most people value.

THE BODY IS A SACRED GARMENT; IT IS YOUR FIRST AND LAST GARMENT: IT IS WHAT YOU ENTER LIFE IN AND WHAT YOU DEPART LIFE WITH AND IT SHOULD BE TREATED WITH HONOR.
~ MARTHA GRAHAM

Emotional Abundance

Emotion is Energy in Motion. It is our body's signaling system and what makes us unique as human beings. Emotional abundance is rooted in unconditional love of self.

Emotion evolves from a sense of connection and security within ourselves and our relationships with others. Embracing and expressing emotional abundance often requires letting go and forgiving previous pain and resentment. We must be free to express emotions safely, as they are a powerful source of energy that perpetuate specific patterns in our lives.

- On a sensory level, behavior and physiology are the tangible expressions of emotion. There are many identifiable emotions: happiness, sadness, anger, and grief. Everyone is unique in his or her expression of feelings and we learn norms regarding expression of emotions in relationships.

- Each of us has experiences and relationships in which we express and observe emotion.

- We must value and validate feelings as important aspects of our being and encourage their appropriate expression within relationships.

Financial Abundance

Many people associate abundance with material and financial wealth. Our success-driven society and glitzy media portray abundance and success in very tangible, monetary terms. Financial security does bring with it a degree of freedom, but that freedom does not always translate to a sense of abundance.

Financial abundance can be a slippery slope... the more you have, the more you spend. Increasing our income doesn't always get us to the level we expect it to. This process is similar to aging. When you reach a specific number, it never seems to be as you expected it to be. The impact of the increase is often less dramatic than we expect.

Money is only worth what we are willing to invest it in. In other words, money is useless in and of itself; it only symbolizes our capacity to get what we want. (If, of course what we want is a commodity available for purchase.) Though we are all familiar with the old saying, "Money can't buy happiness," that doesn't keep a lot of folks from trying!

- Again, looking at financial abundance on a sensory level, a specific amount of money, for example $1000, is finite.

- Depending on your knowledge and experience with money this may seem like a large amount or a small amount. To a teenager, it is huge; to a millionaire it is pocket change.

- Each of us will make different choices how to spend or invest that money, based on our values. Since I value security and freedom, I tend to invest and save more than I spend. Others choose large homes, new cars, designer clothing and exotic vacations, as desirable investments of capital. Our true values are revealed in how we use our resources

An Attitude of Abundance

Abundance is a symphony of mind, body, and spirit. It is about being true to your heart, embracing what you love, living in the moment, and celebrating your life as it is through each of these avenues and more. Abundance is a connection with spirit revealed through lifestyle and philosophy.

My husband and I have been married for over sixteen years, and share an abundance of love. So much so that we decided years ago we would like to share our love with a child by having a family. After years of not conceiving, we decided to adopt and we continue to wait in faith for the blessing of our baby.

This has been a difficult time for my husband and me, wanting something so badly, yet feeling no sense of control over our ability to have it. Many couples in this situation experience extreme depression, despair, and divorce as a result of focusing on the one aspect of their lives that seems to be missing.

We chose to have a different experience. Not to say that grieving the loss of my fertility and my dream of giving birth to our child is not an ongoing challenge. But this "lack" in our lives led us to focus on and appreciate the abundance in so many other areas of my life:

- My husband and I are vibrant, healthy, and still in love after 16 years of marriage.
- We live in a beautiful home in a safe community filled with caring neighbors.
- Loving family and friends surrounds us.
- We have the time, resources, freedom, and flexibility to explore our hearts' desires.
- We worship freely in a country that sees this and other freedoms as inalienable rights.

Most important, our journey through infertility has strengthened our faith and brought us much closer to God in search of his will for us. This relationship brings infinite peace and abundance to my life.

DO NOT STORE UP FOR YOURSELVES TREASURES ON EARTH, WHERE MOTH AND RUST CONSUME AND WHERE THIEVES BREAK IN AND STEAL; BUT DO STORE UP FOR YOURSELVES TREASURES IN HEAVEN WHERE NEITHER MOTH NOR RUST CONSUMES AND WHERE THIEVES DO NOT BREAK IN AND STEAL. FOR WHERE YOUR TREASURE IS, THERE YOUR HEART WILL BE ALSO.
~ MATTHEW 6:19-21

TRANSLATED IN LAYMAN'S TERMS TO MY NEW LIFE PHILOSOPHY:
THE BEST THINGS IN LIFE AREN'T THINGS!

Time and History are on Your Side

Time is another interesting phenomenon related to abundance. We often feel that we have no free time, yet all time is free. We feel we do not have enough time, yet we have all the time there is. We don't get more time until we use the time that we have. Unlike the compounding, regenerating capacity of money, time cannot be reproduced. Once it is gone, we cannot get it back. And we never know just how much more we have!

CONSIDER THIS: IF YOU ARE NOT HAPPY WITH WHAT YOU HAVE, HOW COULD YOU BE HAPPIER WITH MORE?

YESTERDAY IS HISTORY. TOMORROW IS A MYSTERY.
TODAY IS ALL WE HAVE FOR CERTAIN.
THAT'S WHY IT IS CALLED THE PRECIOUS PRESENT.
~ FROM THE PRECIOUS PRESENT BY SPENCER JOHNSON

Time and history connect us to the roots of who we are and where we come from. Family and friends who have known us for years see a deeper side of us. A sense of shared experience and commitment to the past, present, and future adds richness to life.

I find that over time, my history has woven these principles and experiences together, forming the unique tapestry that is my journey to abundance. I grew up as Missy Thornbury in Cary, N.C., a formerly small community near Research Triangle Park. Though the population has grown from 7000 to over 175,000 in the 37 years since I moved there, I still run into my favorite 3rd grade teacher, Mrs. Williams, in the Kmart parking lot. My best friend, Emily, and I recently celebrated 29 years of friendship. We enjoy jazzercising together and retreating to Ashworth's Drugs to eat hot dogs served by the same women who served them when we were in high school.

My brother lives with his family in the house we grew up in, surrounded by many of the same neighbors. Celebrating holidays with family in this familiar setting creates a unique experience. Though many things have changed through the years, abundance flows from my sense of community and shared history in Cary. It always warms my heart to hear someone call me Missy Thornbury, because I know immediately they share that history.

Believing is Seeing

What we believe becomes our paradigm or frame of reference. As a result, we gravitate toward and focus on information that supports our reality. The universal law of resonance confirms that what we focus on expands. Translated here, we see more of what we believe there is to see! We tend to find whatever we focus on.

One of the most classic examples of "Seeing is Believing" is the Rosenthal study. As a result of a computer glitch, teachers were told that specific groups of children were exceptionally bright, or below average. The teachers responded accordingly, and though there was actually no significant difference in the intelligence of the two groups, six months later, the children who were thought to be smarter actually scored higher on achievement tests than those who were considered slow learners. This phenomenon has been consistently documented and is also referred to as the self-fulfilling prophecy.

There is a distinct difference between "Seeing is Believing" and "Believing is Seeing." A classic example of this is revealed through the relationships between Jesus Christ and his disciples. "Doubting Thomas" needed to see and to feel Jesus' wounds before he could believe his identity. The other disciples believed in Jesus Christ and as a result His glory was revealed to them. If you must "see it to believe it" you reveal your own disbelief, which dictates what you are likely to see and believe.

AS A MAN THINKETH, SO IS HE.

~ PROVERBS 23:7

One of my favorite, most tangible examples of abundance is nature, in particular the ocean. Its existence is infinite and I am consistently amazed by its grandeur.

So it is no surprise that in preparation for priming my creativity to write this chapter, I made arrangements to visit my favorite home away from home at the beach. I made my request early, and waited patiently. When word came that my picture perfect beach trip was not available, I was devastated. I thought I had to be at MY beach, in my favorite condo…everything had to be perfect to write my chapter on defining abundance.

Well, I am sure you can see the irony in my story, even without realizing that I live on the east coast, in a state lined with beaches and barrier islands. I can chuckle now when I think of the paradox in my thinking, especially within the context of writing about defining abundance.

Abundance is your birthright, a natural by-product of honoring your spirit and celebrating your life, as you know it. Recognizing and defining abundance is a very personal evolutionary process. Our definitions will change as our lives, attitudes, and experiences evolve. Discerning the difference between WANTS and NEEDS, taking responsibility for your perceptions, and enjoying your life as it is are at the root of honoring your abundance.

I remember a game I played with freshmen when I was an orientation counselor at East Carolina University. I casually passed around a roll of toilet paper and instructed participants to "take as much as they needed." This always proved to be both humorous and enlightening to say the least. Some people rolled several layers around their hands, some took a few squares, some took one and it was not uncommon for someone to pass completely, stating that they had all they needed. Eventually I asked participants to share one piece of information about themselves for each square of tissue they took. You can imagine the laughter and the looks as everyone realized the impact of their perception of need and the responsibility it brings.

YOU GET NO MORE AND NO LESS
THAN WHAT YOU BELIEVE YOU DESERVE.
~ DON MILMAN

YOU CAN'T ALWAYS GET WHAT YOU WANT,
BUT IF YOU TRY SOMETIME, YOU'LL FIND, YOU GET WHAT YOU NEED!
~ THE ROLLING STONES

My sincere thanks to you for your interest in my definition of abundance. I trust your experience has been worthwhile and that your own definition continues to evolve. I challenge you to examine your life through your lens of abundance and adopt an attitude of gratitude. Make conscious distinctions between wants and needs. Simplify, live in the moment, and trust your heart and you will experience the essence of this timeless truth:

IT IS NOT WHAT WE HAVE BUT WHAT WE ENJOY
THAT CONSTITUTES OUR ABUNDANCE.
~ JOHN PETIT SENN

Godspeed in your quest for abundance.

About
Gail Ostrishko

Gail Ostrishko, a creative free spirit, specializes in nurturing individuals and organizations to tap into and radiate their internal wisdom through unique interactive learning experiences. Consistently noted for her high energy and infectious enthusiasm, Gail's light-hearted approach to revealing the infinite wit and wisdom of life is engaging, empowering and fun. Anchored by a core belief *that the best things in life aren't things*, and grounded in years of experience as a counselor, facilitator, and coach, Gail's gift for recognizing, articulating, and applying universal principles through personalized experiences is unparalleled.

A proud graduate of East Carolina University, Gail's degrees in Psychology and Human Development/Family Relations provide a firm foundation for her commitment to facilitating personal and professional growth in herself and others. She is a Licensed Professional Counselor and a faculty member of the William Glasser Institute for Choice Theory, Reality Therapy and Quality Management. She also facilitates career development seminars, feedback, and career coaching through The Highlands Company. She is an active member of the National Speakers Association and the North Carolina Association of Personal and Business Coaches.

Gail continues to evolve as a speaker, author, facilitator, and coach reaching a wide range of clientele through various venues. Ranging from inspiring keynotes and corporate seminars, to intimate retreats and life coaching, these lively learning experiences are guaranteed to engage your mind, body, and spirit in a very powerful and permanent way. Gail's life quest is to be a role model and a resource for loving and living true to your spirit.

Her most powerful calling is volunteering as a wish granter and speaker for the Make a Wish Foundation of Eastern North Carolina. This role engages her nurturing spirit and creative energy to provide powerful personalized experiences for some very special children and families.

Gail enjoys being outdoors and soaking up sunshine. She especially loves flowers and the beach, Jazzercize, and playing the guitar. Also known as the former Missy Thornbury from Cary, N.C., Gail lives in Apex, N.C. with her husband Gary, and faithful canine companion, Casey.

Please visit Gail at www.gailo.com to learn more about her lively learning experiences and products. This chapter, along with others, is available on audio. Projects in the works include two more books, a game, and an audio series. Consider joining Gail and other kindred spirits for the Living and Loving Your Life retreat offered on the private and pristine coast of North Carolina. She can be reached at gail@gailo.com or (919) 779-6546

The Art of Receiving

By Stephanie McDilda

At one discouraging point in my life, I realized that I wanted a lot, but wasn't getting much of it. Most of us desire abundance, but the fact is, we block the flow of what the universe has to offer. Without a doubt, most of us want to attract more into our lives... more money, more love, more joy, and more time.

What we fail to recognize is that we often ask for good to flow into our lives, then we block that good. Why do we do that? For some of us it may be fear that we might fail, or worse, that we may succeed beyond our wildest dreams. Some of us are plagued by self-doubt: " I'd love to go for it, but I'm not good enough, I'm not ready, I'm not worthy." Many people are unfamiliar with the universal laws of attraction. They fail to understand what attracts abundance and don't understand that they may, in fact, be pushing it away. For some it is simply a lack of attention to opportunities. I learned long ago that I had to get out of my own way if I wanted abundance to flow to me.

Many years ago, I heard a joke about a young woman who asked God to let her win the lottery. Week after week, she begged, telling God how good she had been and how much she needed the money. Finally after several weeks, the clouds parted, and the Almighty, in frustration, yelled down, "Give me a break. At least buy a ticket."

In January, I received an e-mail that was sent to all coaches in our area by a retreat coordinator at a local athletic club. They were seeking a coach to do a session at their retreat. While it intrigued me, I thought, "No, they will probably pick someone else." I closed the e-mail and was about to delete it, when suddenly a voice spoke up in my head and said... "Give me a break. At least buy a ticket." I realized, once again, that I was standing in my own way. I had nothing to lose by sending in a proposal. Two weeks after I sent the proposal, the coordinator contacted me and the opportunity was mine!

If you will learn to get out of your own way, you will be amazed at the abundance flowing into your life. In this chapter, I am going to give you some keys to get you started.

Being Open to Receiving More in Your Life

A few years ago, I had an experience that changed my understanding of abundance and receiving. My Yoga teacher sent out her quarterly e-mail announcing the start of new classes. I was short on funds at the time, so I sent her a brief note explaining that I would not be able to afford to attend class this quarter, but I would appreciate it if she would keep me on her mailing list. The next day I received a note from her telling me that she had missed seeing me in class, and that I should pick a 10 week session that she would like me to attend free of charge, as her guest. I was so surprised, that I didn't know how to respond. I do remember thinking that this offer was so generous that I couldn't possibly take advantage of her in this way. Instead, I simply shut the e-mail and went to bed. The next morning, while I was meditating, I heard a very distinct message in my heart. It said, "How can I bless you when you are not open to receiving?" I was shocked when I realized that this was just one more example of how I was blocking my abundance.

How do you respond when someone offers to do something incredibly nice for you? Do you turn them down, saying, "I couldn't impose" or, "I couldn't let you do that"? Instead, why not simply say, "Thank you." or, "I'm overwhelmed by your generosity—thank you."

When a friend attempts to pick up the check at dinner or lunch, do you attempt to wrestle it away from them, or cause a scene by attempting to stuff money into their pocket? Instead, offer a mild protest if it makes you feel better— something like, "Oh, thanks, but you don't have to do that," or, "Please let me, you paid last time." If your friend still insists, very graciously say "thank you."

When a friend gives you a compliment, do you minimize it or brush it off? When they compliment your tie, do you say, "What, this old thing? I've had it for years."? Or is a compliment of your accomplishment tossed away with your reply that, "It was nothing."? Be aware that what you are mistaking for modesty is actually a slap in the face to the person who has just given you a compliment. Not only do such responses minimize the other person's kindness, they also generate negative energy.

Spend some time in the next week observing how often you push away the good that is flowing to you. Keep a running log of all the times you have to remind yourself to "buy a ticket." You will be amazed to find that it may be a habit that runs very deep inside of you.

Sometimes we become fixated on how good will come to us, and where it will come from. Give up the need to control how, where, and when your abundance will flow. When we stay narrowly focused on one source, we are not open to our abundance flowing from other sources. We begin to see ourselves as the source of our abundance. Learn, instead, to see the universe as the source of your abundance. Your job is only one way that money will flow to you.

Remember, too, that money is not the only measure of abundance. At one point in my life, I was very "cash poor." It was at that perceived low point, however, that I realized how truly blessed I was. I may not have a lot of money, but I have the most incredible family and friends. I have more love than any one person should expect. While work was slow, I had the most wonderful abundance of time.

A year ago, I started an activity that you may find enlightening. I call it the "Pennies from Heaven" log. In a ring notebook, make a log with three columns. The first column is for the date, the second for the amount, and the third (and largest column) is for an explanation. As soon as you have started your notebook, take note of EVERY blessing that flows to you. I have even recorded finding a dime in the parking lot! This log should not only reflect money that comes to you, but money you save as well. I once saved $34 with grocery coupons and my store MVP card. Boy, was I jazzed! Since I have started using my log, I have received free Yoga classes, free personal training at the gym, free coaching, free copies at Kinko's, free lunches and dinners, free movie theater tickets, a free visit to the dentist, and free concert tickets to see Neil Diamond! The key to using this log is to reflect, with gratitude, on every single thing that comes into your life and to realize how much of it comes from sources other than yourself.

Remembering that you will receive many blessings from the universe that have nothing to do with money is also important. Start keeping a gratitude journal, and make note of those things. As you pay attention to them and feel your gratitude growing, you will note with interest that the rate at which they flow seems to increase.

If you find that you have hit a negative slump, and can't seem to shake it… I have been there, too. Here is my favorite remedy. Get a small spiral notebook—one you can easily carry in your pocket or purse. If you carry a day planner, you can use that instead. At the top of the page, write the date and number the page from 1-10. During the day, write down 10 good things that happened to you today. Do this every day, and before long, it will seem easy. When it becomes easy, increase your goal to 15 things or 20 things. Soon, you will be focusing on the positive things in your life rather than the negative and you will be opening yourself to receiving more of them.

Clarifying Your Vision

We often state our wishes and desires in very general terms. "I'd like more romance. I'd like a better job. I'd like to be happier." Attracting something to you is difficult if you are not clear about what you are seeking. The clearer you can be about what you want in your life, the more you will be able to focus your energy into intent rather than wishes.

Several years ago, I was working in the Training Department of a large company. Although it was not my official capacity, word got around that I had a background in Career Development. Individuals would often come in my office, sigh, and say, "I hate my job." "What would you rather be doing?" I would ask. The most common answer I received was, "I don't know, but I hate this job." (I should note that this was not a statement about this particular company. Some reports state that as much as 65% of American adults hate their job.)

Start by identifying what you want. Openly brainstorm everything that your heart desires. These desires could be physical (I'd like a new red Porsche), emotional (I want more joy in my life), or spiritual (I'd like to have purpose in my life). Don't be censored by "shoulds"—in either direction. Don't pursue something you think you should want, like a promotion or a specific career choice, if that decision does not inspire you. On the other hand, don't eliminate something from your list because it doesn't seem right or proper, like lots of money or a life of leisure. If you have difficulty deciding what you want, start with what you don't want and convert it to a more positive description.

Be specific about what you are seeking. "A new job" is not specific. You do not have to know at this time that you want to be a CPA with a specific firm (unless that truly is the identification of your dream). If you don't have a name for what you want, start with the characteristics. "I want a job helping people. I'd like flexible hours and the ability to work from home. I want a job with low stress that will allow me time with my family."

Put your feelings into this exercise. Feelings are the language of your soul and they carry some very attractive energy. Identify how you believe that you will feel when you reach your dream. The more specific you can get about your vision, the more you can visualize the outcome. When you can visualize the outcome, you will start to get excited or experience joy. As you generate this energy, you will begin to attract your desires in your direction.

Be very careful to stay away from feelings of frustration or lack, which come from your not having attained your goal —yet. These negative feelings of lack attract more lack. This is a universal principle. Instead, find ways to focus on the things you already have to feel good about. Take your focus away from what you don't have, and keep it on what you intend to have.

There are several things you can do to make your vision seem more real and to start the flow of positive energy. If you are visually oriented, get a large piece of poster board and make a collage that represents your goal. Cut pictures and phrases out of magazines, use computer clip art, and draw, if you are artistic. This is not only fun, but it can get your creative energy flowing around attaining your vision. Once your collage is completed, put it where you can see it every day.

Perhaps it takes only one piece of visual stimulation. When I decided I wanted a new car, I got a brochure from the dealer, and looked at it every day until the car was in my garage. One day, I would like to have a vacation home in the beautiful North Carolina mountains with a spectacular view. While I was on vacation, I took a gorgeous panoramic picture of the mountains from the Blue Ridge Parkway. That picture is now on my bulletin board with the caption, "View from the Deck."

If you are verbally oriented, try journaling about your vision with vivid detail. Describe your dream as if it has already come true. Include as much detail as you possibly can muster. Yes, this is a creative writing activity in the largest sense! If you want a trip to Europe, describe it as if you have been. Talk about where you went, what you did, what you saw, how you felt! The key is to get as inspired and excited as possible. Flow that positive, creative energy toward your vision and it will flow back to you.

Make Space in Your Life

Only a few years ago, I was holding the desire for new clients in my business. Then I realized, if they did call, I wouldn't have any space on my calendar to work with them. My life was full, but many of the things it was full of were not the things I wanted. If you are feeling overwhelmed, your conscious mind might be saying, "send me more," but your subconscious will be stressing over how you will manage, and will push those things away.

A well-known characteristic of physics is that nature abhors a vacuum. Start now to get rid of what you don't need or want in order to make room for what you do want. As you start to eliminate the things that don't serve you, you will be creating that vacuum, which will draw in the things you want.

The easiest place to start decluttering your life is in your physical space. A client of mine was preparing to hire a Feng Shui expert to organize her home and office. "Let me save you some money," the Feng Shui expert advised her. "Before I come out and charge you by the hour, clean all the clutter out of your space." You may not see how cleaning out your closets will increase your ability to receive more in your life, but once you try it, you will be surprised at how amazingly free, light, and upbeat your energy feels. Start with the closets, and the cabinets. Don't forget the attic, the garage, the workshop, and under the beds! Clean out your wallet, or your purse. Purge your file cabinets and your Rolodex. When you think you are done... clean out your car, including the trunk! Make a huge pile of things you haven't used in a year or more. Then make a decision to sell it, donate it, trash it, or for special reasons, to store it away neatly.

The next place to start decluttering is in your mental space. Being organized and using a planner is a big weight off of my mind. When I write things down, or know where they are, I don't have to worry about them. Learn to be gentle with people, but ruthless with your time. Identify your priorities and stick to them. Learn to say "no" to things that don't fit for you. Imagine how much negative energy you generate when you resent doing something to which you wish you had said no. Refuse to invest your time in things that don't energize you. If you wish you had more time, take a look at how you are spending (or wasting) your time right now and eliminate those things from your life. A friend of mine once commented, "I don't know how you have time to get so much done." My response to her was, "I don't know how you find time to watch television." Television can be educational, entertaining, and relaxing. If it isn't, turn it off!

Another way to declutter your mental space is to live in integrity and tell the truth. Integrity is that place that joins who you are inside with how you behave outside. If you say your family is a priority, and yet you spend excessive amounts of time at work, you are out of integrity, and it will weigh heavily on your mind. Speak your truth always. If you stop telling lies, you never have to worry about being found out, or about sustaining your story.

Perhaps the hardest space to declutter is your emotional space. Let go of relationships that do not nurture or honor you. If the relationship is important to you, set boundaries and communicate those boundaries to the people who are not respecting them. If they value you, they may be willing to change, but remember—you cannot change another person. If they are not willing to respect you, leave them behind and move on. Make space in your life for people who will love and respect you. You deserve better. Consider, as well, letting go of emotional baggage. Seek counseling if necessary. Learn to forgive those who have hurt you in the past and move on with your life. Learn to respect and love yourself. See yourself as healthy, whole, and totally worthy. You are.

One of my favorite exercises for making space in your life is to make a list of those things that drain you and then systematically eliminate those things from your life. Include things in your physical, mental, and emotional space. Include little things like squeaky door hinges, a dirty spot on the carpet, or a burned out light bulb. Don't be afraid to include big things that seem too difficult to tackle, like my home is on a small piece of property and my neighbors are too close. Work on what you can, and let the universe handle the rest. Soon, you will be freeing up space for wonderful blessings to flow into your life.

Give Up Thinking that it is Better to Give Than to Receive

As you were growing up, someone—or a lot of someones —told you that it was better to give than to receive. Those who seek to receive are thought to be selfish or self centered, and surely doomed to spend eternity in someplace unbearably hot. Let me pose this question to you. If we are all giving, and no one is receiving, to whom are we all giving?

Many years ago, a dear friend of mine offered to extend to me a generous favor. As was my habit back then, I declined and said, "That is too generous. I can't accept your offer." Suddenly, she blurted out angrily, "How dare you! How dare you deny me of an opportunity to be blessed?" I was shocked, but I suddenly realized that she had done me an even bigger favor with her comment.

To give is not more blessed than to receive. Giving and receiving are reciprocal parts of the same cycle. If you do too much of one and not enough of the other, the cycle is thrown off. In order for you to be blessed by giving, someone must receive. Occasionally, you must do the blessing and play receiver to someone else. This is a matter of balance. The intent of our early lessons was to keep us from becoming greedy and selfish. The result was to throw the balance off in the other direction, and make us feel that we should be doing all giving and no receiving.

Here are some reasons why it is also blessed to receive:

- Your act of receiving brings great joy to the giver. Think about it. How did you feel the last time that you did something nice for someone? Excited? Joyful? Warm and fuzzy? Receive with enthusiasm and you will give those same feelings to another.

- God intends for you to receive abundance. It will come to you in many ways and from many sources. If you refuse to receive, you are denying God's blessings.

- Receiving, especially things like love and care, enables you to be a better giver. Mother Teresa once said, "In order to keep the lamp burning, you must keep putting oil in it." If you want to be there for others, you must occasionally be there for yourself, and let others give to you.

- Receiving allows others to open the flow of grace to themselves. As the saying goes, what goes around, comes around.

- Your willingness to receive can teach your children to give.

Giving is good, too. Don't forget these are balanced parts of the same cycle. If you want to receive something, learn to give it. One of my clients said that he didn't feel appreciated, and wished that people (at work and at home) appreciated him more. I asked him when was the last time that he gave appreciation to others. Although he felt that he did better than his co-workers and friends, he had to admit he was a little lax in the appreciation area. I asked him to find five people to appreciate in some way each day. Within a matter of weeks, he noticed that other people were starting to appreciate him as well. Try this exercise. Make a list of things you would like to receive. Pick one, and start to give that same thing to others. Keep a journal of what you are flowing out, and what flows in to you. When things flow in to you, be open to receiving them—in whatever form they may show up. Remember... it's a cycle.

Practice Gratitude

There are few emotions as attractive as gratitude. Think about the last time that you gave someone a gift. Did they thank you, get excited, use it, and enjoy it? Or, did they barely acknowledge it, act bored or blasé, and leave it in a drawer or closet? How did their response make you feel about giving them a gift in the future?

Translate that to a universal perspective. Do you recognize the gifts the universe is giving you? Do you say thank you, get excited, use it, and enjoy it? If not, why expect more?

The universal law of attraction says that you get more of what you focus on. You will attract positively or negatively based on your emotional vibration. If you wish to receive more good in your life, you must be a positive vibrational match to all you wish to receive.

Try these ways to have and express more gratitude in your life:

- Keep a gratitude journal.
- Make a standby list of things you are grateful for and when you feel down, pick one item and focus on it all day.
- Identify your blessings and gifts and determine how you will use them. When my grandmother died, she had a closet full of gifts still in the boxes. When you die, will your gifts still be in the box?
- Appreciate others.
- Get the Thank You habit. Recognize all of the things you take for granted. Thank God for the sunset, the bird songs, the green traffic light, and any other thing that comes your way and makes you smile.

- When you experience something that you perceive as bad, write it down and follow it with a list of ten things that are good about it.

The more you can find to be grateful for in your life, the more you will receive things for which to be grateful.

Your greatest block to your flow of abundance is your unwillingness to receive it. We ask for good, and yet when it comes to us, we deflect it out of guilt, or we overlook it because it doesn't appear as we expected. Be open to every opportunity that comes. Be willing to receive your good in a form other than what you expected. Get clear on what you want and make room for it by getting rid of what no longer serves you. Balance the cycle of giving and receiving and be grateful for absolutely everything. And, if you want to receive more, give the universe a break. For Heaven's sake… buy a ticket!

About
Stephanie McDilda

Stephanie McDilda, M.Ed., is the President of Success Basics, a firm specializing in authentic power, leadership development, and interpersonal relationships. Stephanie balances her time between personal and professional coaching, corporate training, and keynote/motivational speaking. Her energetic and personable style puts people at ease and keeps them involved.

A graduate of North Carolina State University, Stephanie holds an undergraduate degree with a double major in Business Management and Economics. She also has a Master's degree in Adult and Community College Education (1990) and a Master's degree in Counseling (1997), both from N.C. State. In August of 2000, Stephanie completed her professional coach training through Coach University.

For 15 years Stephanie worked in a corporate environment, holding several management positions, facilitating management and interpersonal skills training, and coaching managers. Since starting Success Basics in 1993, she has been privileged to provide training and coaching to a wide range of individuals from Vice Presidents to Administrative Assistants... and a whole host of wonderful and fascinating "characters" in between. Her specialty areas include authentic power, life planning, balance, personal leadership, professional development, spiritual growth, management/leadership development, and resilience.

Although her background is in career development, Stephanie prefers to take a life planning approach with her coaching clients. She believes strongly in their holistic growth, because there is not one part of you that is not connected to and affected by every other part. She enjoys working with individuals who are spiritually connected and are seeking meaning and purpose in the framework of a balanced, joyful, abundant life.

To contact Stephanie, call (919) 212-0098, send an e-mail to smcdilda@successbasics.com or visit her website at www.successbasics.com.

The Powerful Seven Steps to Magnetic Abundance

By Cathy Nealon

Would you like to give up the struggle and spend less time and energy trying to make things happen in your life? Wouldn't it be great to have all that you desire come to you? Not only is it possible, the good news is you already have all the necessary ingredients to make it happen. All you need now is the recipe, which you will find in the powerful intentioning process outlined in this chapter.

Intentioning is the process of becoming a powerful magnet to attract all the abundance you desire and deserve. The intentioning process focuses on developing a plan to help you:

- discover your essence
- identify empowering actions to manifest your desired outcome
- create space to allow abundance into your life
- learn how to trust and let go of the outcome
- gain the principals and skills to keep you focused in the present
- have all the abundance you seek find you

We spend much of our life collecting different components and ingredients, including our thoughts, dreams, beliefs, interests, strengths, and values. We then spend much of our finite time and energy in this increasingly faster-paced world trying to figure out how to integrate these ingredients to bring us meaning and purpose.

At a certain point, many of us come to realize that we each have all the power we need to manifest the things we desire in our lives. Only in the last decade did I become more consciously aware of just how powerful a creator I am; that I always have been; that we all are. Like Dorothy in the Wizard of Oz. She spent time seeking the formula and direction for her happiness in the world around her, only to learn that she had the power within herself all along.

In this chapter, I will outline The Powerful Seven Steps to Magnetic Abundance. This amazing process will give you the skills and tools you need to identify and integrate your unique ingredients by taking self-empowering actions to define and manifest abundant living in your life. By following this recipe for your own success you can more easily direct your life and have what you desire start coming to you.

The Powerful Seven Steps to Living an Abundant Life

1. Start with a Pure Heart

> "WE RECEIVE THINGS WE PREPARE FOR."

The first step in living an abundant life is to understand the natural process of intentioning. Intentioning begins as a seed. The seed is your plan you use to design what will give you meaning and purpose in your life. You choose the seed. You just need to be clear if you want to become an apple tree, a beautiful wild flower, or some other fragrant bloom.

To identify what seeds you want to plant, begin by defining your essence—things that give meaning to your life and represent goodness, wholeness, connection, and completion for you—what your heart desires. The more specific you are, the more you will get what you truly desire. This important step begins with knowing that one can only intention things that are free, things that are not attached to or belong to another. To do this, you will need to go within. Typically your head holds your wants, needs, doubts, and fears, while your heart holds your desires, things that bring you joy, peace, and fulfillment. When you follow your head you will likely get more wants, needs, and fears.

Going within is simpler than you think. Let's begin by playing one of my favorite games—the Association Game. To find the answers to these questions, close your eyes and focus on one question at a time. Closing your eyes will allow you to get out of your head and open the door to let your heart guide you. The game is called the Association Game because you identify the first thing that comes to you, no thinking allowed. This provides you with a way to feel, taste, and see what is really important to you.

Ready? Name the first car that comes to you when you close your eyes. What color is it? Although you may share a similar answer with someone else, what type of car and color you choose will likely mean something different to you. What is important to you is not always what is important to others; it is, in fact, what makes you unique. It is your truth.

So what car and color came up for you? Ask yourself what your answer means or represents to you? How did it make you feel? Is this something important to you? Do you want more of this in your life? Marilyn, who recently completed this exercise, identified a green Volvo. To her, the car represented safety. Green reminded her of nature and being nurtured, like new green leaves in spring. When I asked her if safety, nature, and being nurtured were important in her life, she said they were very important components, and that she wanted more of those things in her life. Now try this with other parts/components of your life and see what comes up for you.

Another simple exercise is to identify your heroes and state what you admire about them. You may find that you admire a particular person or a group or category of people. For me, I admire anyone who has had to overcome hurdles in their life. I personally admire their courage and strength. They are qualities I continue to want to expand in my life. This exercise can help you see who you are becoming, the space you want to step into, or what you want more of in your life.

By following these simple, yet effective exercises you can:
- examine what is important in your life
- begin to articulate and express your unique truth
- decide what seeds you want to plant

The next step is learning how to prioritize and integrate the planting of your unique seeds by finding and creating the right action steps that will work best for you. The actions you choose will determine how to nurture your seeds so they can bloom and bring into your life all that will make you happy and complete.

2. Visualize the Outcome

"BEGIN WITH THE END IN MIND." ~ STEPHEN COVEY

Clarity is power. The more specific you are in discovering *who* you are (your values, strengths, natural talents, and abilities) and *what* you enjoy (your interests, skills, and accomplishments), the clearer you become in identifying your unique recipe. These ingredients provide us with our roots. When you follow what you are naturally drawn to, you gain more alignment, meaning, flow, and ease in your life. Our main mission in life is to be happy, and the only way we can be happy is by being *who* we are.

By completing the exercises in step one you are now clearer about what you value and the areas of your life you want to expand. Next, let's look at a few more reflective questions and simple exercises to help you further define your unique recipe.

Define Your Unique Gifts and Interests

- List three things you loved doing as a child and ask yourself what gifts you received from them? How did they make you feel?
- List three accomplishments you are proud of? Ask yourself how these made you feel?
- List three skills or areas of interest you want to expand. Ask yourself what these will give you?
- List three of the happiest times in your life. Ask yourself what was it that made you happy?
- What is your message? What do you want to share with others?

- What is your legacy? What do you want others to say about you on your 80th Birthday?
- Make a list of things you want to do before you die.

One of the most important realizations I discovered when doing this exercise was that as a child I loved taking different scraps and threads to create beautiful clothes for my Barbie dolls. From this, I learned that I love to make something out of nothing. I found that one of my key talents, an important component of my essence, is I have the vision to see the big picture, as well as the ability to integrate, synthesize, and blend the many threads and ingredients available to create something new, simple, clear, and transferable.

You have now identified the ingredients that make you unique in your life—your interests, gifts, and desires. The next step is to integrate and blend these into your unique recipe.

One of the most important elements of a successful corporation is the clarity of their mission and vision, of who they are, what they want to accomplish, and where they are going. How many of you have examined these areas in your life? Do you have a clear mission statement and vision for your life?

To start the next exercise, review all your ingredients to find any repetitive patterns or recurring themes. Then fill in the blanks below.

Your Personal Mission Statement

My mission is (to bring, to use)_____
(Objective - your unique talents, abilities, skills, interests, etc.)

To (do, be) _____
(What you desire)

Result _____
(Impact/contribution/accomplishment)

Cathy's Sample Mission Statement

My mission is to integrate and share (my objective) all my abundant blessings, lessons learned, life experiences, and tremendous skills to be a beacon of light (my desire) to help illuminate the way so others can find their way home to the truths within themselves to become happy and complete once again (the result).

Now that you have more clarity about *who* you are and *what* you want, it is time to prioritize and focus on the areas of your life that you choose to expand. You can use the following Life Balance Exercise weekly, monthly, or periodically. I personally find that it works best for me to set and achieve quarterly goals.

"What You Focus on Expands."

"Setting Priorities in Your Life is the Key to Succeeding."

Life Balance Exercise

Instructions:

Rate your satisfaction on a scale of 1–10 (10 being highest) on where you feel you currently are in each category per the descriptions given below.

On the same scale of 1- 10, rate where you ideally want to be in each area.

Choose three areas as your top priorities—areas you want to focus on **now** in your life. Only choose three, because what you focus on expands.

On a separate page write what your ideal life/wishlist would look like in these three areas. Be as specific as possible. Include what it will look like when you achieve all that you are looking for, how it will feel, and what your environment will look like. Check to make sure it is aligned with providing you more of what you value and desire.

Create three action steps you can take to close the gap from where you are to where you want to be. Take a moment to reflect on what you have already done to get to where you are today in each area. For example, if you are a six in personal development and seek to be a nine, spend a moment reflecting on what you did to become a six and from there create three action steps to help you move toward your goal of nine. Make sure you include a timeframe for accomplishing each action step in your plan.

Life Focus Areas	Where are you today?	Where do you want to be?
Finances Your comfort with giving & receiving money.		
Personal Development Your growth and self-discovery process.		
Physical Well-Being Your body, health, personal safety.		
Physical Surroundings Your home, office, car, etc.		
Primary Relationship In/not in a meaningful one-on-one relationship.		
Profession Utilizing your unique gifts and talents.		
Relationships Satisfaction with family, friends, associates.		
Rest & Relaxation Time for you to regenerate, enjoy, and have fun.		

By visualizing and clarifying your desired outcome and by creating the empowering action steps to attain your outcome, you have begun the very powerful process of creating a magnet, a powerful force that will pull you toward making your goals and desires materialize in your life. Remember to begin with the end in mind because without vision or direction in our lives we will perish.

Now that you have become clear on what is important to who you want to become, you now need to create the space to make it happen.

3. Letting Go - Ridding Ourselves of Attachments

"It is through creating, not possessing, that life is revealed" ~ Vida Scudder

We have become *who* we are by our attachment to *what* we have been exposed to. Many of our beliefs come from our teachers, parents, mentors, and others who have crossed our path. Without questioning the beliefs we have been exposed to, we repeat the cycle and project those beliefs onto others in our lives. If one grew up during the depression, one might have a frugal outlook on life; if one grew up in a very rigid environment, one might project their version of doing it "their way" onto others. If one grew up without all the nurturing and support they yearned for, they might project feelings of not feeling "good enough." Others may have been exposed to a fear-based environment where risk was not encouraged, so "status quo" might become their norm.

Interpreting these beliefs is not about judging whether these beliefs are good or bad. What is important is deciding what is good for you. So many of our repeated messages and inner negative voices come from limiting beliefs. Looking at our thoughts presents us with an opportunity to take a look at what we have personally been exposed to and ask if this belief reflects *who* we are and *what* we want more of in our life today.

We nourish our thoughts by paying attention to them. Remember the Patrick Overton quote "Watch your thoughts, they become words. Watch your words; they become actions. Watch your actions; they become habits. Watch your habits; they become character. Watch your character; it becomes your destiny." What you put into something you get back. For example, if you were to save money, you would reap interest. If you were to plant an apple seed, you would get an apple tree. When you sow negative thoughts, you reap more negative thoughts. As things we reap build on each other they become our template for what we attract in life. Everything in life is a mirror. *You are what you attract.*

Have you ever felt that you in fact created the event, situation, or particular thing that appeared in your life? For example, have you ever been thinking of someone and they called you? Or have you ever felt that something wonderful was going to happen in your life, and it did? Sarah Hughes, the gold medal winner of the Olympic figure skating experienced this. She knew from a very early age that she would some day win the gold medal, and she did.

Have you ever had a day full of chaos? Have you ever stopped to ask yourself if this could be a reflection of what you were thinking? Have you ever felt that you couldn't make a decision because your thoughts were congested, then found that you have developed a cold? Everything in life is a projection of who we are and how we feel. When we do not feel good about ourselves, we attract others to us that also do not feel good about themselves. When we do not respect ourselves, we attract people who treat us poorly. The outcomes—the effects—we produce in our lives are directed from what we believe—the cause.

Have you found yourself being fearful of something, to find that it actually manifested in your life? A recent story I read exemplified this. A man named Matt and his friend drove over an embankment and landed overturned in a brook. As it filled with frigid water, Matt had to pull the friend from the vehicle to save his friend's life. The interesting part of the story was that Matt revealed that he had always had a fear that something like this was going to happen. Could it be that he had manifested the accident happening?

Fear is a common attachment that drains our energy. Fear puts us in a self-made prison, when it results from a personal choice. Fear typically signifies to us that we have a lack of reserves in another area of our life. If fear is consuming us, we have little or no room to move forward in life, because we only have a finite amount of energy and reserves. When we embark on making changes in our lives, the fear increases. The bigger the change, the greater the fear. To take back the control to direct our lives so we can move forward again, we need to make something larger so we can make the fear smaller. To give up our attachment to fear, we need to put our focus on identifying and taking the action steps that will move us forward in our lives. Each empowering step will build on the last, creating momentum. This momentum then creates a powerful magnet that will pull you toward achieving your goals and away from the fear.

Another huge attachment drain in our lives is creating expectations. An expectation is a personal attachment to an outcome, something we take ownership of, something we choose to hold onto. Simply put, expectations are about others—expecting someone else to do something. By doing so we give away our power, depleting our energy reserves even further. For example, have you ever been disappointed when you did not get the gift you were hoping for, but didn't ask for, on your birthday? Even though most of us know that by creating expectations we will very likely be disappointed, we continue to create them because of our conditioning. So ask yourself, what is it costing you to be right? To have it done your way?

Letting go of expectations is like the serenity prayer: "God grant me the serenity to accept the things I cannot change (others), the courage to change the things I can (myself), and the wisdom to know the difference."

Abundance is simply a conscious choice. Do you choose to live in lack or abundance? Do you prefer to be right or happy? Do you ask why, instead of why not? Do you say, "I have to" instead of choosing the actions that will move you forward? Do you choose to say, "I don't have" instead of asking, "what can I do"? Do you settle for things in your life or do you create a plan to improve your life? You see, abundance is our perspective—and perspective is our choice.

Are you ready to put the brake on lack in your life? To let go of the excuses and attachments that have kept you stuck? Are you ready to seek to understand others, not change them? Are you ready to listen to the wisdom of your heart and let go of the fear in your mind? To choose to spend your time looking for opportunities that will energize and not deplete you? They will find you, if you let them. Are you ready to decide whether it is more important to win the battle or the war? To stay stuck in being right, having it your way, or having the bigger more rewarding life you are truly seeking?

By ridding yourself of negative attachments, you can end the depleting and exhausting cycle of lack in your life by gifting yourself with an abundance of new space to create and attract more of what you want and what is important to you. Remember, what you sow, you reap. Choose to sow positive thoughts and watch as you reap all the abundance that will make your heart sing. Now that you've looked at what you can let go of, let's look at the nurturing steps you can take to begin to manifest your desired outcome.

4. Live in the Present

"THE PRESENT IS PERFECT."

Your personal power is always in the present and *"Now"* is the time to step into your personal power. If you choose to live in the past with the "I could've, would've, should've's," or in the future with the "I hope, I wish, I want's," you are giving your power away. The past is over and you have no control over the future. If you put your focus on the past or the future, you will miss all the abundance and gifts awaiting you in this moment. If you choose to sit back and not direct your life for yet another day, you will find yourself repeating the same patterns over and over again. You will continue to live your life on automatic pilot, with the "I have to's" instead of the "I choose to's." You will then find yourself asking how did I get here again? How did this happen?

The truth is, living in the present is your choice. Choose to live your life today and be present in the moment by connecting with all that is important in your life. One of the reasons 12-step programs are so successful is because they put their focus on living in the present, one day at a time, one moment at a time because that is all that is in one's control. In this section we will focus on some ways you can achieve this.

One of the most important areas you can put your energy and focus into is taking the action steps you created in the Life Balance Exercise. By placing your energy on things that are in alignment with *who* you are and *what* you want and letting go of old habits and beliefs, you reduce your resistance, thereby increasing the pull to accomplishing your results. Taking actions in the present gives us clarity, and clarity gives us power.

Accepting yourself for *who* you are and where you are going is another powerful way to stay grounded in the present. Always remember that the present is perfect. Know that each event and situation that presents itself in your life is there for a reason. So look for the opportunity, the gift being presented in the moment. Know that where you are in your life is where you need to be. If you find yourself feeling rushed or feel that you do not have the time to get everything done, you may want to adopt one of my favorite expressions someone once shared with me: "Time will expand to meet my needs." Every time I use this expression I am amazed that everything falls into place so easily and effortlessly, once I let go of the outcome.

The easiest and most powerful way of staying focused in the present is by having an attitude of gratitude. By stopping during our day to take gratitude breaks, we experience more richness, beauty, and expansiveness in our lives. We can do this upon waking in the morning, while we are driving or commuting to work, while we are eating, in our conversations with others, before we go to sleep at night, and in every part of our waking day. A wonderful way to practice gratitude on a daily basis is by keeping a gratitude journal. This is a place where you begin or end your day with all that you are grateful for. Or have you ever just made a simple list of the things you are grateful for? If not, take a moment now and see how easy it is to list over 100 things that you are grateful for in your life today.

With gratitude and humility, embrace all the fullness and blessings life has to offer. Look for the gift being presented in all things. By doing these things, you are directing and creating the life you choose. By following these steps you are stepping into and becoming the best you can be. You are creating a bigger and more powerful magnet that is pulling you closer and closer to making your dreams a reality.

Now that you can see how important staying in the present is to stepping into your personal power, the next step is to transform your intentions, your unique goals and desires, into reality by learning how to manifest them with faith and trust.

5. Learn To Trust With Faith Not Fate

"What You Believe You Will Achieve."

Trust begins with humility. Trust is believing in something greater than ourselves. Trust creates an opportunity for us to surrender to God (our higher power, the universe, a source greater than you), and with a pure and humble heart ask for what it is that is sought. God only wants to gift us with all that will make us whole, happy, and complete. The gift is God in action. Aren't you comforted to know that you do not have to do it all, and that you don't have to do it all alone? How blessed we are that God is our abundant and endless source of supply.

Trust begins with you. Trust is not something you inherit, it is something you learn through your experiences in life. A few years ago I had an incredible experience. I was in a head-on car collision on a snowy road in Pennsylvania. This was symbolic of what was happening in my life. What I call my vertical life (living from the inside out with my values and interests) was in collision with my horizontal life (my external life, my career). The message was clear as soon as the accident happened. The message was about trust; that it was time for me to let go of the identity of *who* I had become. It was time to leave my career of 22 years. As I had followed and completed all the steps in the intentioning process, it was time for me to trust that the universe would gift me with what I would be doing next. By becoming clear on the components of *who* I am and *what* is important to me—my unique ingredients—I did not need to have the answer. Instead I needed to trust that the answer would find me. When I let go of trying to figure out what to do next, Coaching found me.

Trust is having faith. Faith provides us with the assurance of things to come; it is a belief we direct with confidence, a conviction of believing things not seen. Faith is a proactive way of achieving your dreams; of doing what you can do to prepare for and stay open to receive.

The opposite of faith is fate. Prior to my car accident, I believed that I was trusting in my life, as so many wonderful things came to me. I then learned that fate is a blind assumption that everything will work out. Fate is sitting back and waiting for something to come; being complacent, not choosing to direct our lives. Fate is not seeking what is really important to us and aligning our lives with the essence of those things. Fate is accepting whatever we get in life. Since the car accident I have chosen to proactively direct my life and now all the abundance I've sought has found me.

Some of us use fate as an excuse for not moving forward in our lives. Sometimes we hide behind fate when we feel we may not be deserving of the things that will bring happiness, joy, and contentment to our lives. If you find yourself here, I encourage you to take out a sheet of paper and make yourself an "I Deserve List." Make the list as long as you can. As you write, remember, your birthright is to be happy and joyful. Your responsibility is to ask for what you desire. For it is in asking that you receive.

Faith is believing that all things are possible. Remember the little girl played by Natalie Woods in the movie "Miracle on 34ᵗʰ Street"? What she desired more than anything was a big, beautiful home in the suburbs. Although learning to trust was something new for her, she continually repeated, "I believe, I believe, I believe," and her dream house appeared. Continue to have faith and believe. Have faith because when you do, miracles happen.

Now that you have strengthened your trust muscle, you will now learn how to affirm your desires as a way to keep you grounded in faith through trust in action.

6. Affirming Your Desires

"It is Already So."

We state our desires with affirmations. They can be negative or positive. Powerful affirmations are positive statements made in the present tense. They are typically short and focused on what we desire to achieve. They are tools we use to direct our beliefs. They are like a bridge. They help us get from where we are to where we want to be. They are a very effective and powerful way to recondition our negative thoughts and limiting beliefs by turning them into simple, positive, results-oriented, true statements.

Affirmations are a confirmation that what we desire and deserve is already happening. They can be likened to prayers, as they are a way to communicate with our creator, the universe. They provide us with a way to express gratitude for what is to come. And gratitude is a way to keep us grounded in our faith that our intentions are happening.

Powerful affirmations have three important components:

- The first begins with gratitude. Begin each affirmation with an offering of gratitude for what you are seeking.

- The second component is your message—the essence of your request—what you desire, stated in the present tense.

- The last component is focused on a short statement made with conviction that shows that the answers to your requests/prayers are being confirmed. My favorite is "it is already so."

Sample Powerful Affirmations

Gratitude	Intention, Request, Essence of Message	Confirmation
Thank you	Something good is going to happen to me today	It is already so
Thank you	My life is overflowing with abundance	It is already so
Thank you	I am now directing my life with ease and in flow	It is already so
Thank you	I am open to receive all the blessings I deserve	It is already so
Thank you	I am open to new sources of income	It is already so

Use your own words in each of these three sections to create powerful affirmations for yourself. Affirmations are most powerful when you write them out and repeat them often throughout your day. Take a moment now and write out a few powerful affirmations for you to manifest the desired outcomes you identified in the Life Balance Exercise in Step 2. Place them on index cards and put them in visible places where you can see and read them during your day. Consider placing them on your bedroom or bathroom mirror or in a prominent place on your desk, or maybe on your refrigerator. Remember what you focus on expands so repeat them often throughout your day.

Now that you have affirmed your heart's desires with gratitude and faith in you, you will now focus on ways to ensure that what you ask for, you will receive.

7. Prepare for the Gift of Receiving

"Do unto others as you would have them do unto you."
~ The Golden Rule

To prepare to receive, you first need to understand the cycle of giving and receiving. You cannot have one without the other. The cycle is a continuous flow. Always ask yourself, "what am I receiving from those to whom I give?" Ask yourself what you have to give those from whom you receive. A very simple, yet powerful example is when you take a moment and share a great big smile with someone you do not know. Who is actually receiving the gift? How do you feel when you see the impact you had on this person when you see their face light up and smile back? How do you feel when you see how much joy you brought into someone's life by doing something so simple? As St. Francis said, "It is in giving, we receive."

Whatever you send out to the universe will come back to you in greater proportion at a later date. There are no exceptions. If you send out lack-based thoughts and beliefs, then you will get an abundance of lack in your life. If you choose to be complacent and do nothing, then you will reap a whole lot of nothing. If you are a taker, then more will be taken from you. Our actions always mirror our intentions and they are increased by the universe and returned back to us with interest. The longer it stays out there, the greater the interest. So choose to be discriminating in what you want returned to you.

Receiving can sometimes be harder than giving. As many of us have been conditioned to be givers and caretakers, especially women, it becomes more difficult to break out of this mold and put ourselves first in our lives and become more open to receive. How comfortable are you when you receive a compliment? When someone acknowledges something you accomplished, are you open to receive the gift or do you minimize it by saying it was no big deal? We need to remember that if we do not receive the gift presented, we break the cycle, canceling the gift given. By staying open to receive, we then have the ability to acknowledge the gift, its intention, and the giver with gratitude, which is our gift back to them. Receiving genuinely with our hearts is a display of humility and love. Sometimes it is only in the eyes of the receiver that givers discover their gifts. Receiving is a way to invite others into our lives. The gifts we receive shape *who* we are.

The Summary of the Powerful Seven Steps to Magnetic Abundance

"Our life is a gift from God, what we choose to do with it is our gift to God."

This comprehensive intentioning process allows us to see time and again that we are all-powerful creators. We direct and create the life we choose; what we believe we will achieve. What we focus on expands, so by choosing to follow The Powerful Seven Steps To Magnetic Abundance you can now begin living the life you have been yearning for. As you continue to build your intentioning muscle, you will more easily and effortlessly attract the prosperity and abundance you desire and deserve.

Start with a Pure Heart:

Seek your truth and follow your heart. Find the essence in all things. Make conscious choices to direct your life. Choose only those things that will bring you energy and joy. Remember, you receive what you prepare for.

Visualize the Outcome:

Clarity is power. Create a mission statement for your life. Always begin with the end in mind. Prioritize what is important to **you**. Create a wishlist and a self-empowering action plan for your life. Never focus on more than three things at one time. Always have a timeline for each item to pull you toward making it happen. Invest in you by aligning your life with **who** you are and **what** is important to you. Set your sights high based on your unique truth, not others.

Letting Go - Ridding Ourselves of Attachments:

Let go of negative attachments to things that are untrue and do not serve who you **are** and who you are **becoming** (old beliefs, fears, excuses, expectations, etc). Choose how you want to respond to each situation in your life. What you sow you reap. Let go of being the judge and reacting to things, as it blinds you from being focused on what you desire and deserve.

Live in the Present:

Put yourself first on your priority list. Expand your awareness and see the greater possibilities. Tap into your personal power by stepping into and living the life you were born to live. Complete the self-empowering action steps you created to move you toward your goals. Stay focused on your path and enjoy the journey. Keep your words focused in the present (I choose, I claim, I am, I direct), so you do not cancel what you are striving to achieve. Keep focused in the present with a positive attitude of gratitude. Don't shoot the messenger. Know that the present is always perfect.

Learn to Trust – Faith vs. Fate:

Trust is having faith. What you believe you will achieve. Believe in You. Choose to take the driver's seat and direct your life. Meet your goals half way. With humility, realize that you are only part of the answer. Let the universe gift you by surrendering the outcome (the how, the answer). Let go and let God, our endless source of abundance, gift you. Get ready to watch the miracles unfold in your life.

Affirm Your Desires:

Affirm your heart's desires with gratitude and faith in you. Start each affirmation with gratitude. Be clear on the essence of your request. Be careful of what you ask for. End your affirmation with confirmation and conviction ("it is already so"). Place your affirmations prominently where you will see them each day. Repeat them out loud often throughout your day. Do not settle for anything less than you deserve.

Prepare for the Gift of Receiving:

Be open and receive with gratitude. Give what you want to receive. Walk your talk. Mean what you say, say what you mean. Live your values. Celebrate differences. See the divinity in others; let them see the divinity in you. Get the support you need to succeed. Find others to hold your intentions. By combining your intentioning power with others it will increase the power of your intention. Surround yourself with people you admire and have what it is you seek. Always be authentic and celebrate *you* for being the magnificent, unique being that you are.

By combining all your unique life ingredients and integrating them with this powerful intentioning recipe you have now become a very powerful magnet. The rewards and results will now find you. Enjoy your newfound abundance, flow, and prosperity.

In closing, remember the only one who can make you happy is you. Gandhi said, "Your life is your message." Make yours count. Erma Bombeck said, "At the end of my life, I would hope that I would not have a single bit of talent left and could say I used everything God gave me."

Create a great life **NOW**. Only *you* can.

About
Cathy Nealon

After 22 years as an Executive Sales Director for a Fortune 10 Company, Professional Life Coach Cathy Nealon now pursues her passion by helping others find, achieve, and maximize their personal and professional potential.

Cathy found the recipe for success and abundance in her life by integrating all of her tremendous life lessons, rich life experiences, and learnings. She created Amazing Possibilities Life Coaching in 1999 as a way to give back and share her recipe for success. Through the use of guiding tools, life skills, and coaching principals, she helps her clients shorten their cycle to finding their unique path to achieve all the abundance they desire and deserve in their lives.

Cathy completed the Master's level Spiritual Coach Training program at the Coach For Life Institute and is currently enrolled in the Coachville Graduate School of Coaching. She is also a member of the International Coach Federation (ICF).

She co-created a community-based coaching program called The Coaching Connection, which provides tips, tools, and skills to all those interested in becoming the best they can be personally and professionally. In addition to co-authoring a monthly column and a free monthly newsletter she is a talented speaker, facilitator, and retreat and workshop director.

With Cathy's warmth, integrity, enthusiasm, and sincerity, she has helped many individuals find their path to making empowered decisions. Her expertise lies in her ability to inspire people to discover their strengths and become motivated to improve the quality in all areas of their lives. Her coaching specialties include:

Executive Coaching: Utilizing a results-oriented approach, Cathy helps her clients create win/win meaningful workplace environments. She also partners with entrepreneurs to provide them with the support they need to succeed.

Co-Creation Coaching: Cathy helps clients clarify their vision and dreams and translate them into executable plans to make them a reality.

Connection Coaching: Cathy helps many clients become all they can be Personally and Professionally by helping them discover and design a unique blueprint for their success.

Women in Transition: Cathy enjoys supporting women in finding their truth and wisdom in all types of personal and professional transitions.

Cathy lives in the beautiful White Mountains of New Hampshire. To contact her, call (603) 383-3639 or to sign up for the free Coaching Connection newsletter, email Cathy at cathy@amazingpossibilities.com or visit her website at www.amazingpossibilities.com

The Problem of "Not Enough"

By E. Thomas Costello

We already have abundance! We are experiencing the <u>exact</u> amount of abundance that we allow ourselves through our beliefs, attitudes, and consciousness. Our current view of abundance is simply an indicator of where we are in our journey from separateness to wholeness. When we focus on the distance between ourselves and what we want, we reinforce our view.

Thus, we create our "level" of abundance. Taking responsibility for where we are at this moment is very empowering. We can choose to be grateful for where we are. Instead of complaining about our situation, we can acknowledge the "facts" about it and look for other choices to set the stage for moving forward.

Abundance can be defined as having choices regarding how we want to Be, Do, and Have. When we feel limited in our choices, we experience lack, the opposite of abundance.

Abundance is more about Being than Having; more about realizing than acquiring. Abundance is a matter of perspective. The following story illustrates these ideas:

A father of a very wealthy family took his son on a trip to the country to show him how poor people live. They spent a couple of days and nights on a farm of a very poor family. When they returned home, the father asked his son, "How was the trip?"

"It was great Dad!" the boy replied.

"Did you see how poor people live?" the father asked.

"Oh yeah," said the son.

"What did you learn?" asked the father.

The son answered, "I saw we have one dog and they have four. We have a pool that reaches to the middle of our garden and they have a creek that has no end. We have imported lanterns in our garden and they have the stars at night. Our patio reaches to the front yard and they have the whole horizon. We have a small piece of land to live on and they have fields that go beyond our sight. We have servants who serve us, but they serve others. We buy our food, but they grow theirs. We have walls around our property to protect us. They have friends to protect them."

With this, the boy's father was speechless. Then his son added, "Thanks Dad for showing me how poor we are."

There is always a different point of view. Sometimes in our struggle for "net worth" we forget what really matters most is our happiness in life.

How We Process Information

We live and build our lives according to our beliefs. To "get" abundance, we need to start by working on those beliefs. The conditions that exist in our lives are the result of how we process information. For example, if we are financially secure, chances are we process financial information effectively. If there is an area of our lives that is less than abundant, it is safe to say that how we process information contributed to the creation of that situation. To experience abundance in our lives, we must process information effectively.

Processing information involves being able to separate the facts from the "story." Facts are observable and accurate. The story consists of our interpretation, made up meanings, and significance that we have attached to the facts. The interpretations are often not accurate, but we treat them as if they are. Therein lies the problem. If we have interpretational filters on, we can distort how we perceive and process information. The filter referred to in this chapter is the "I Am Not Enough" filter. This filter decreases our information processing effectiveness.

The "I Am Not Enough" filter is put in place very early in life, perhaps at birth. It may occur when we recognize that, in comparison to others, we are smaller, weaker, hungrier, colder, or wetter. The filter might also occur repeatedly in our childhood when the world reflects our "Not Enoughness" back to us by the way we are treated or mistreated, respected or disrespected, etc. The "I Am Not Enough" filter distorts incoming data. Someone's harmless glance gets interpreted as an insult directed at us. Actions or inactions on the part of others are processed as painful stabs, even though there was no such intention.

"Not Enough" thinking is my description of what I see as the underlying problem with people and how we perceive ourselves. "Not Enough" thinking is the opposite of "Abundance" thinking.

When we believe in something untrue such as "I Am Not Enough," we tend to react in several possible ways:

- We try to overcome this curse by working compulsively to prove it wrong.
- We succumb to that belief and act it out in a dramatic way in order to prove it true.
- We use some substance or activity to alter the mood associated with this painful belief. Cigarettes ("I'm not relaxed enough"), alcohol, drugs ("I'm not at ease enough"), caffeine ("I'm not energetic enough"), diets ("I'm not thin enough"), work ("I'm not achieving enough"), sex ("I'm not attractive enough"), and food are popular distracters. Obviously this approach causes more problems than it solves.
- We use interpersonal strategies that seem promising, but yield no results, or even negative results. As we try to get what we want through manipulation or trickery, we fail, and by doing so frustrate others and ourselves.

The Basis of Abundance

The basis of abundance is our relationship to what we want and to what is possible. When we consider the object of our desire, we can determine our relationship to it by noticing the emotions that spring up. We can feel we are "less than," "more than," or "equal to" our desired condition. The lack of abundance can be seen when we don't have the proper relationship to what we want and when we don't recognize that a better condition is even possible. Said another way, we either think we are limited (Not Enough) or the choices are limited (Not Enough). In abundance thinking, neither of these views is evident.

How to Know When We Are Moving Toward or Away From Abundance

We can represent ourselves in relationship with other people, activities, and ideas by using circles in a diagram. For example, if we feel we are "less than" someone or something else, we can represent this relationship with us in the Little Circle (LC) and the other in the Big Circle (BC).

If we minimize them and inflate ourselves, the circles are reversed with a "more than" attitude represented by the BC and a "less than" position (LC) for them.

Both of these scenarios are fear-based. The fear is that there is not enough for us both to have something. There is "Not Enough _____ " (fill in the blank), so either they can have "it" or I can have "it."

The Equal Circles (EC) represent the condition of mental, emotional, and spiritual equality even if the physical equality doesn't yet exist. By this I mean that we can be excited about this condition—even grateful for it—although we may not yet be in physical possession of the object we desire. We trust in the possibility that it will be ours. There is no mystery

that the Equal Circles are in fact larger than the Big Circle since almost no effort is expended on protecting one's holdings or degrading another's position.

When we are Equal to what we are thinking about, working toward, looking at, or talking with, we are, in effect, reducing the distance and difference between it and us. We don't focus on the difference or distance, or how hard it is to achieve or obtain this item or condition. Our focus is more positive. Instead of being Little Circle, "it is so far for me" or "it's too hard to get" (victim-like), we are at ease with the idea of having this condition.

We are not in the Big Circle, blustering about not wanting whatever we don't have or actually being afraid we can't achieve it. Instead, we are willing to be in the same space as the object or condition we desire. We are Equal to the situation or object or condition. When the EC occurs, you will experience a pleasant, relaxed face with excited and accepting feelings in the stomach and chest.

The Little Circle

With the Little Circle (LC), there is a noticeable pit-of-the-stomach shrinking. We tend to feel smaller than we actually are. We feel unable to deal with the situation, condition, or object at hand.

The LC is that attitude developed by a child who makes a comparison of his/her self to an adult's self. The conclusion reached is, "I am little and they are big." The comparison can be made between size, power, freedom, self-determinism, or other facets of identity. Children can start with "I Am Not Enough" in terms of how tall, how strong, how free they are to move, to decide, etc.

From this "condition" the child then develops a set of tactics to use when it wants something. Calling attention to its need for food, dryness, love, etc., may take the form of crying, screaming, laughing, tantrums, anger-like behavior, and so on. The behavior is as if the child were looking through a magnifying glass at everything. Problems are seen as large. Challenges are seen as large. Authority is seen as large.

This point of view has significant positive value. It can help people avoid, figuratively speaking, head butting a locomotive or rhinoceros. It can help us to perceive danger and the risk inherent in a situation. It serves to reinforce caution, and encourage planning and preparation.

The downsides include leading us to feel helpless, quit, underestimate our talents, fail, avoid challenges or responsibility, self-sabotage, not ask for what we want, not take care of ourselves, have a sense of not being deserving, low self-esteem, "hiding our light," see opportunity as danger, or not reaching higher. Another major downside is when we blame others for our feelings and make them the problem.

We learn "skills" as children to get others to do what we want. We apply those "skills" as we get older. Unfortunately, they are not necessarily the most effective way to get what we want.

The judgment that " I Am Not Enough" sets the pattern in motion. While I've outlined the downside, there is an upside to feeling "Not Enough." The upside is that, if looked at in a healthy way, it can lead us to find constructive ways to deal with these feelings and thoughts. If we are 90-pound weaklings, we can exercise to become bigger and stronger.

The Big Circle

When we are in the Big Circle (BC), the fear of inadequacy frequently manifests as a face-thrusting-forward posture of attack. We suddenly become the expert in whatever the subject is, we shout, use abusive language at times, and do whatever it takes to "be in control" of the situation, condition, or object. We are afraid. We rebel and resist in reaction to a threat. The BC would rather fight than to flee. BC people can be angry, chip-on-the-shoulder-types who are constantly locked in a battle with control. Control is generally interpreted as authority. They are against authority.

Big Circles have victim-like characteristics since they are reacting to an externally defined agenda. The BC's seem to think that being against something is the same as being for another thing. It is not. "Being against" says that the opponent has determined the field for the battle. "Being for" is to have chosen your own field for the game of your choice. The BC has victimizer tendencies. By victimizing someone else (usually a Little Circle) they reinforce, at least temporarily, their sense of being "Enough."

Big Circles appear to be looking at themselves through a magnifying glass. They are larger, or so it seems. This adolescent overestimation and self-puffery distorts reality by minimizing the risks of a situation relative to their own capabilities. Not that Big Circles are courageous. They are not. They can be foolhardy. They can be bullies. They are desperately trying to prove something, namely that they are "Enough." In this context, Big Circles can be particularly dangerous in a gang of their peers, each trying to prove "Enoughness."

Big Circles have learned to use their intellects to keep their emotions isolated. "Getting into one's head" and staying there limits the "dangers of emotional involvement." Emotions are often seen as weaknesses. Not being able to control their emotions leads them to isolate or compartmentalize their emotions. They don't listen. They don't take advice. They may not wear seat belts. They may not obey speed limits. Snobbery can be very Big Circle-like.

Trying to prove we are "Enough" is not necessarily bad. What is bad is when our proof requires that others be made less. We can take steps to prove we are "Enough" without minimizing others.

The Little Circle position is fearful and initially yielding. The Big Circle position is fearful and initially aggressive. The Equal Circle position is more accepting, less reactive, more loving and balanced.

What Has All This to Do with Abundance?

We can literally feel our relationship with what we want. When we focus on a desire and feel positive feelings (of love or attraction) for it, we're likely to be in the Equal Circle. We are apt to gain those things we love.

Love has been defined as attention (seeing things as they are, without judging), respect (not changing people or things; not intruding upon or interfering with), and appreciation (not devaluing another, their gift, or oneself). Having love in our lives is an indication of abundance. If we become Little Circle or Big Circle when considering what we want, we are still operating in the realm of "Not Enough," or the opposite of abundance.

Abundance is a point of view just as scarcity is a point of view. One can build the case to support either one. Since abundance is what we are trying to get, why not build a case for that? Take past experiences or current conditions and convert them into value. This removes the negative emotional charge from those things we may be using to keep ourselves away from abundance. This will also help us overcome "Not Enough" thinking and operate in Equal Circles in relationships.

Ideas to Overcome "Not Enough" Thinking

1. Tell the truth about this issue in your life.

Do you frequently judge yourself as wrong or "less than" or "more than" others? Do you feel victimized by life or experiences? Do beliefs that you are not smart enough, thin enough, rich enough, strong enough, young enough, educated enough, etc., hold you back? Consider the possibility that you are hurting yourself with other peoples' words and attitudes. Make other choices. Write down the "facts" of your situation to make sure you are not confusing the "story" with the "facts."

2. Grasp the concept of "untruth."

This idea can be expressed in a variety of ways: erroneous core beliefs or a "bug" in the human computer, etc. The point is that influential ideas you believe to be true about yourself are not true! For many, navigating life's paths with a compass where north, south, east, and west are inaccurately placed leads to a lot of unnecessary struggle. Become aware of which beliefs you hold about yourself that are not true.

3. Get a coach or a mentor.

Using a guide is not a new concept. Guides, coaches, mentors, teachers, et al. have been around for centuries in all cultures.

4. Recognize the spiritual element in your life.

For many the ultimate magnetic north on their compass isn't north at all. It is the force that they recognize as the Creator behind all that is. By developing and being aware of this connection, you can learn you are never alone or lost.

5. Work at staying in "Equal Circles."

Notice the relationships in which you adopt a childish pose that is inferior (the Little Circle). You feel you "have to." Big Circle is the superior view where you feel "I don't have to!" This rebellious attitude is designed to regain control. "Equal Circles" is when you have a choice. "Control over" is no longer the goal. The sense of equality reduces stress and leads to a greater sense of respect, attention, and appreciation. Watch how you think, feel, and behave for hints on this idea.

6. Disconnect from people who deliberately try to put you into the Little Circle.

We often see an untruth that says, "My greatness is contingent upon your smallness." People who believe this are motivated to keep you small. Beware!

7. See your emotions as your greatest allies.

Consider that your emotions (and your body's other signals) are nature's way of giving you gauges on the dashboard of your life. Be eager to look for the message they are trying to convey. Emotions have unique characteristics. They have positive, empowering messages that guide us toward constructive action. Knowing your emotions, what messages they have for you, and what actions you are being guided toward gives you powerful resources other people deny or are constantly at war with.

8. Disclose what you have been keeping secret.

John Bradshaw, celebrated author, says, "We are only as sick as our secrets." Untruths hide in the darkness of our secrets. When we bring them into the light, their hold over us is lessened. Compassion seems to be a natural byproduct of disclosure. Disclosure can help another's compassion grow, just as it can increase our lightness.

9. Develop a relationship with someone who mirrors your "Enoughness."

The person who sees the world as a half-empty glass is not likely to see you any differently. Find someone who mirrors your finest qualities and for whom you do the same. Here's a clue: Do you like whom you are when you are with them?

10. Give positive value to events that you may be holding in a negative light.

Everyone has had negative experiences in their lives. To continue to be a victim (Little Circle) to this event is disempowering. Finding meaning or value is a way to become Equal to the event. This will allow healing.

11. Invest in yourself first.

Eating right, exercising, personal care activities such as haircuts, etc., are important to your self-care. Be sure these activities are not quick fixes or addictions, which are not investments.

12. Journal out of the Little and Big Circles.

Use a journal to write out and bring light to your thoughts and feelings. This sets the stage for you to make other choices as to how to think and feel. Journaling is one of the greatest tools for self-discovery!

Reasons Why Someone Wouldn't Get What They Want

1. They don't really want it.

Sometimes the lips say one thing and the heart and head say other things. Some of our "wants" come from others and we are not committed to them.

2. They benefit too much from their current situation to change.

There are often "payoffs" that are so appealing that giving them up is frightening. These benefits should be reexamined to see if they are self-empowering.

3. They think they are "not enough" to get it; they are not equal to what they want.

The "deservingness" issue is very powerful. On the other hand, as Napoleon Hill said, "What the mind of man can conceive and believe, it can achieve." Because a goal is active in your consciousness, you can grow to be able to achieve it.

4. They perceive dangers to getting it.

With the mixed signals we've received about money, success, looks, etc., some people may worry about their own behaviors, souls, and families should they get what they want. This can be especially true if they have been taught that they are basically bad and life is about controlling their badness.

5. They don't realize what their current situation is costing them.

Often when a person sees limited choices they don't see the upside they are passing up. As the life they want comes into focus, so does the gap between where they are and where they want to go. The gap can shed light on the costs.

6. Getting it would violate their values.

Similar to #4, this really reflects a set of limited choices and limited vision. For example, while "money is the root of all evil" is a judgmental term applied to money, great good can come from the use of money as a tool. If our religious upbringing painted money as evil we are likely to have internal conflicts about acquiring it.

7. They believe that they deserve what they now have.

Not only can the deservingness issue, as in #3, limit the upward reach of a person, it can also lock them into the condition. This is where punishment can be the purpose of staying in a bad situation.

8. They have not bothered to really define what they want.

It takes time, effort, and introspection to get at our true values. Without this investment, we can be influenced by spur-of-the-moment urges. We can miss fulfillment and satisfaction by chasing "empty calorie" activities.

9. They don't understand how things come to be created.

There is a process of how things get from the invisible to the visible, from the thought to the material plane. For example, children may think money comes from wallets, pockets, and pocketbooks. Some adults can think money comes from a company or the government. Still others believe that creating value can create money.

10. Talking about it is easier than working at it.

If the goal of having a goal is getting attention, then just talking about the goal can produce that result. If talking about it produces the reward of attention, why jeopardize that by taking responsibility for actually achieving the goal? A symptom of this condition can be "big talk, no action."

11. Their energy flow is disrupted so they sabotage their own efforts.

Despite all the talk to the contrary, there are "invisible" shackles, resistances, and obstacles preventing constructive action. There can be a huge internal battle between the desire to do something and the desire to avoid doing that something. Worst of all, most of this is below the person's awareness. That is what makes it so frustrating. "I can't understand why I can't accomplish this!"

The field of Energy Psychology, which includes Emotional Freedom Techniques (www.emofree.com), deals with this fascinating area of enhancing human potential.

What follows is a way, along with Emotional Freedom Techniques to release negative emotional energy, to shift "Not Enough" thinking, which will facilitate our experience of abundance.

A Process to Bring Abundance Into Everyday Life:

1. Write a story, with as much detail as possible for those areas in your life where you want to experience abundance more fully. The story can be about a goal, desired outcome, objective, or want in an area. The areas could be: Spiritual, Mental, Emotional, Physical, Career, Family, Financial, Social, Leisure, and Community. Plan to edit, embellish, and refine this story over a period of time. You are literally creating your life experiences.

2. Write down all the ideas, judgments, fears, beliefs, resistance, doubts, etc., that you have about your goal and that area of life _and_ everything you have heard about

it. Do this in a short, hectic pace, say 5-10 minutes, writing as fast and being as thorough as you can.

3. Identify the one sentence in your list that most states that "I am not sure I'm _____ enough to _____." This "wall" separates you, and in a convoluted way tries to protect you, from your goal.

4. Write out where this idea could have come from. Consider that those sources were projecting their own sense of "not enoughness" rather than seeing yours.

5. Write down the "value" or benefit to you and others of your being a victim (in the Little Circle) to this idea.

6. Write down the cost to you and others of your being a victim to this idea.

7. Write down the "value" or benefit to you and others of your being antagonistic (in the Big Circle) to this idea.

8. Write down the cost to you and others of your being antagonistic to this idea.

9. Identify the value or benefit to you and others of you getting what you want (Equal Circle).

10. Identify the cost to you and others of your getting what you want.

11. Decide. Then enjoy your life of abundance!

About
E. Thomas Costello

E. Thomas (Tom) Costello has been involved in metaphysical, energy issues, human motivation, and coaching for performance since 1969, when he was taught "automatic writing." Since then he has pursued his inquiries into "what makes people tick," knowing there is much more than meets the eye.

Tom's coach-specific training comes from Coach University, Coachville, and from being a student of two terrific coaches. He recently became a Certified Life Purpose and Career Coach from the Life Purpose Institute in San Diego. Looking back, he sees that coaching is what he has always expressed and sought.

When Tom wanted to move beyond processes aimed at accountability, structure, and willpower, he sought to deal with issues at a deeper level. Over the last few years he has trained in Emotional Freedom Techniques (EFT), Tapas Acupressure Technique (TAT), Be Set Free Fast (BSFF), and Psycho Energetic Auro Technology (PEAT). These techniques provide ways to recapture encysted energy. By dissolving "logjams" (blockages), we can again access that energy, eliminate painful emotions, and gain new confidence and certainty about our lives and ourselves.

Tom has a business and military background, including sales and management in small and Fortune 500 companies. He was a partner and general manager of a telecommunications company in California, and spent six years in the United States military, attaining the rank of

Captain in the U.S. Army Special Forces (*Green Berets*) after enlisting as a private.

After working for the Dale Carnegie Institute in sales and as an assistant instructor, Tom spent years exploring self-improvement philosophies and religions. He also read about and extensively studied the factors that contribute to human motivation and behavior. Tom is a serious student of metaphysics and spirituality. For 15 + years he has coached with a metaphysical approach.

Relationship coaching and the personal issues that either boost or hinder accomplishment are Tom's specialties. The impact that self-awareness has on clients, their families, their associates and their achievements excites him. He coaches people to focus on and utilize their strengths, not dwell on their weaknesses.

Personally he is sensitive, intuitive, compassionate, and empathetic. Criticism, from self and others, is a major component of people's "untruths" about themselves. More criticism is not the solution. Seeing other choices and knowing how we decide gives us the tools to create the life we want.

Tom's other works include the first in a series of children's books called "Johnny Proboscis And His Four Extraordinary Pals."

Tom was born in Greenport, New York on the eastern end of Long Island and has lived all over the U.S. and Panama. He is fluent in Spanish, having trained at the Defense Language Institute while in the military, and attending military school in Colombia as a U.S. Army officer.

Tom is married to his childhood sweetheart, Mary Ann (after being apart for 35 + years). They have four children, six grandchildren and two stepchildren. They live in Kansas City, Missouri.

To contact Tom, send an email to tcostello@kc.rr.com or call 816-746-0115.

Principles to Access the Flow of Abundance

By Claire Walsh

Just as the ocean splashes against the jetty creating a spray of bubbles that think they are alone and separate until they fall back into the sea, we often think we are alone and separate from all that's in our lives. I find comfort in knowing we're not!

That thought came to me when my husband and I were standing on a cliff in La Jolla, CA in 1987, watching the waves crashing against the embankment. I pulled out my 35mm camera loaded with 400 film, and positioned the lens for f-stop 1000 to catch the crushing waves at a standstill. Little did I realize until I developed the film that the bubbles were suspended in mid-air like they had no connection to the ocean. But I knew better. And I thought that we too could at times feel disconnected from our Source. And how little we know or understand about the truth of our connection to the greater consciousness that knows how to fulfill our needs.

If we knew we were connected to that greater whole, if we knew our source of "abundance" were in the consciousness that knows, and that we don't have to DO anything to access it, would we be so frightened? Would our decisions be based on fear? Would we run forth with our lives creating magic and living our destiny, or would we, like the clam washed up on the shore, close ourselves off? I think if we only knew and truly believed the power of our connection to that source, there would be no question about our abundance; we would feel tremendously peaceful, connected, and prosperous in all areas.

Why do some people seem to have great abundance and others seem to always struggle just to get through each day? How can you access the flow to abundance so you can experience more?

Abundance is not just for people with a given talent or an inborn skill. Having what one desires is not a lucky break that happens to some and not to others. Each person has the tools to create what they want. Within each of us are the answers and talents we need to create unlimited abundance for ourselves, and to have what we need both physically and spiritually in all areas of our lives. However, abundance is more than just having things; it is also having a feeling of fulfillment. So how does one access abundance?

I found out quite by accident how abundant my life was when I noticed how my life was working with very little conscious effort or struggle on my part. I became more conscious of the principles that contributed to the flow, and how, when I ignored those principles, the flow stopped. The more I lived by these principles, the more I realized I had more control over creating abundance than I originally thought possible. How was this so? Aren't things really out of our control? Isn't there a greater force that is responsible? Do we really have the power to create our abundance?

Let me clarify that, just like the bubbles I saw on the jetty have all the components of the vast ocean, we too have all the components of the greater consciousness that some call God, Source, Higher Power, Higher Self, Buddha, Life Force, or Divine Intervention. Therefore, in a sense, we create our own abundance. But we don't do it alone. By opening up to receive and accepting what is, we attract things to us much like a magnet draws certain objects to it. However, a magnet can only pull toward it a substance that has the right components. A magnet does not attract wood or cloth or plastic. Likewise, we only draw toward us that which is within us. Simply said, **we have to be what we want to attract**.

If you don't like what you are attracting, change your thoughts and beliefs. You cannot attract things unless they are within you. If you are unhappy, you will be surrounded with sad events; if you are negative, you will create negative images and circumstances to reflect that negativity; if you are judgmental, you will always feel judged; if you are critical, you will be criticized. The good news is that it works in a positive way as well. If you are loving, forgiving, and nonjudgmental, people who love and support you, who are not critical of you, and who are forgiving of your shortcomings will surround you.

So how does one begin to access their intrinsic, abundant nature? I believe there are six main principles to help you access the flow of life to more easily attract what you want and to manifest an abundantly rich life. These principles will help you to open up and receive that which is already there.

The Three Legs of Commitment

Abundance begins with commitment. There are three parts to commitment, and like a three-legged stool that collapses if one leg is missing, so too are these three pieces essential and intertwined. If you are not committed, nothing happens. Likewise, commitment opens the flow that makes everything else possible.

Commitment to You

The first "leg" is commitment to you. Have you ever seen a successful person not really care about what they were doing? Could you imagine an actress not putting in the hours it takes to research, study, and memorize her roles? How about a singer who doesn't want to spend time training his voice, or a skater who doesn't commit to daily practice of her routines until perfected? Commitment is showing up fully and saying YES to you and what you want. Doing what you know how to do 100 percent, even when you don't have the complete confidence to do it, is commitment. Commitment is about being willing to expand, grow, stretch, evolve, and take risks.

On a daily basis commitment shows up as respecting our bodies by eating healthy, drinking plenty of purified water, taking vitamins, stretching, exercising, not over-committing or over-scheduling, keeping our minds uncluttered and positive, and paying attention to our emotions. In a broader sense, it's stepping into your greatness even though you don't feel so great.

When I hesitantly left my job at a high-tech start up, I knew that I wanted to inspire others to live their best lives, tap into their greatness, and fulfill their purpose. I also knew that coaching was a piece of how I would go about doing that. But I wasn't sure I was ready, and I didn't have the confidence to just go out and start doing it. Not long after leaving my job, I was asked to provide some Human Resources consulting for a small high-tech company. I had never consulted before—at least not in the real sense where you get paid specifically for your direct contribution. I didn't have a consulting agreement, a business card, or a brochure, and I didn't have a plan about what I would consult about. And besides, I was going to be a coach and this didn't sound like coaching. I was fearful, to say the least, but I also knew that I needed some means of support while I developed my coaching practice. This opportunity was being presented to me despite my internal protest, so I said, "Yes, let's talk." I figured I could always turn it down if it wasn't something I could handle. I could always back out, but I should at least give it a try.

That discussion led to a three-month assignment in which I was able to work part time from my home, set hours convenient to my schedule, and earn what I had been making working full time—at a part time rate! Who would have known! I couldn't conceive that one if I tried. The experience all began with saying "yes"—yes to my dreams and me. The first "yes," was when I decided to leave the company, even though I wasn't sure where I'd go or how I'd get started. But I honored and respected myself enough to move on from an impossible situation. The second "yes" was when I agreed to consult, even though I didn't feel like a pro. The fact is that I was committed to my growth and to myself, and was willing to commit 100 percent and to do what was needed to get where I was headed. Staying at the company would not have honored my true self and saying "no" to the consulting agreement would have stunted my growth.

Commitment to Others

The second leg of the three-part commitment principle is commitment to others. When we commit to others, we are also committing to ourselves, because we are all one—just like those bubbles from the ocean. When we commit to others, we show no harm in thought, word, or deed; we suspend judgment and expectations that anyone should ever be anyone other than who they are. Though we don't condone inappropriate behavior, we accept that everyone is doing the best they can in any given situation. We hold up the mirror and see our reflection and we recognize that all relationships are just reflections of ourselves. When our buttons are being pushed, we look within to see the connection. We see others as our teacher and recognize that everyone has within them the power to be a Hitler or a Mother Theresa. We set them free and as we do, we set ourselves free.

Jane, a client, was struggling with a co-worker. No matter what solution Jane presented or what suggestion she made, her advice was always rejected. They always seemed to butt heads, usually ending in a disagreement or silent standoff. Jane was confident her ideas where good, and resented that she wasn't listened to. We talked about holding the mirror and seeing what reflected from within. At first she couldn't see the connection. But once she risked looking at herself, she could see herself in the stubborn co-worker. She then discovered that in her need to always be right, she alienated others and set herself up to be rejected. Understanding that, she started looking at the result she wanted—which was to be heard and have some of her ideas accepted. She realized that by letting go of having to be right and not forcing her opinions, but rather by seeking to find the best solution, she was able to get her ideas implemented. In looking at her co-worker's stubbornness, she saw her own obstinacy and was able to heal it.

Commitment to the Greater Whole

The third leg of commitment is to the greater whole. This part of commitment is accepting the knowledge that we are all connected at a deeper level. We are all part of a greater vision than our own narrow view exposes. We know that there is a purpose for everything that happens, even if we don't understand it. We are connected to our environment, nature, and all living entities. On a daily basis, our commitment shows up as honor and respect for the environment. We recognize a larger purpose and know we have a part to play; we have an obligation to participate fully in life and fulfill our destiny and we live our life committed to the whole.

So how does having commitment impact our abundance? By committing to our self, others, and the greater scheme of life, we affirm our good; we give of ourselves. In giving is receiving. What we sow, we reap. What goes around, comes around. As we commit and show up in all areas, the universe says "yes" to us and returns or reflects back to us what we've given out. Being committed allows us to receive what we have given. Rather than having what we've done come back to haunt us, it comes back to bless us.

Be Present in Every Moment

We spend so much time worrying about the future that it robs us of the present. Being present means not lingering in the past rehashing old issues, or hanging out in the future trying to figure out how things might turn out. Being present is being conscious of everything around us, and using our five senses to experience all of everything in the moment.

Living in the present means that you are not worrying about what will happen next. You know that the present moment creates the next moment and the future. So you concentrate on what you can do in that moment to live fully and completely, and let the rest take care of itself. Where you are today is a result of everything you did in the past.

So, if you don't like where you are, you can change that by living in the present, and in this moment, choosing differently.

The present is perfect for what we need to learn and grow from. However, the present doesn't always look or feel very perfect. Sometimes the present shows us patience, courage, responsibility, faith, or trust. Many of my clients express dislike for their current job or life situation and wish they could move on. But it seems they are stuck and unable to move forward. One client could never find what she felt she was suited for and was frustrated that she was underpaid and under-utilized. We worked on staying present and committing 100 percent of herself to her situation. She started showing up more fully and immersing herself in doing the work to her absolute best. In a short time, she started enjoying her work, and a new opportunity opened up for her.

The present is for living. You can plan for the future while living in the moment, but the key is to not dwell on it—just live for it. The potential for joy, learning, and excitement is in the moment. Don't miss out. Being present allows you to experience the abundance of your life in this moment. Not waiting for more or better things to come your way, but simply enjoying the abundance of your life as it is, right now. Living in the present is realizing and accepting the abundance that surrounds you and that contributes to the ever-plentiful flow, and releasing thoughts that your life should be any different.

Create a Silent Space

Have you noticed how much of your day is filled with noise, chatter, and "busyness"? Do you often find yourself over-scheduling, over-committing over-working, over-planning, and dropping from exhaustion at the end of the day? What will it take for you to slow down and be still for just a moment?

For me, it takes a head cold or disturbing incident that interrupts me enough to cause me to stop and pause. For some people, it takes an illness or accident to get their attention. Still, others keep up the erratic pace, not knowing there is another way. Why do we humans have such a difficult time being still? And what purpose does it serve anyway?

Our Western culture is based on accomplishing things, setting goals, and making things happen. Activity is the name of the game. The more we do, the more we feel like we are doing something. The more commotion we make and the busier we are, the more alive we feel—the more we can check off our unending list of things to do to feel accomplished. "Doing" makes us feel important; things are happening.

So silence is not a universal value. Some may consider it being lazy, wasting time, or a completely worthless "activity." Silence is not highly prized in our culture, so being still is more difficult for us. And for those who have tried it and felt nothing happened, they might still be comparing their experience to others to make sure they are doing it "right" and "getting it."

For those who practice meditation or silence, they know the purpose. There is nothing magical about being still or meditating, except what happens when you do. Often what "happens" occurs later and not necessarily during your silent period. Being silent is a matter of being still and quiet to listen to the small voice within for messages. Solutions appear and ideas are generated in the silence. But stillness is far more than absence of sound; it's the absence of activity and thought. Being still attunes you to your greater depth, where awareness develops, intuition flourishes, gratitude abounds, and flow happens.

In stillness, you move into an alpha state that gives you control over your mental life and access to the continuing experience of flow.

Set Your Intention and Focus

What is your intention and is it in the forefront of your mind everyday, or do you aimlessly wander around with little focus? When you are awake are you clear about your purpose and are you focused on what you want? Is your intent for a day of anxiety and stress, or are you intent on things going smoothly and effortlessly? Are you anticipating that the best will happen, or are you waiting for the other shoe to drop?

An important part of creating abundance is your point of view and belief about abundance. Are you coming from a perspective that the universe is totally abundant—a cornucopia of everything that your heart desires, everything that you need and want is here for the asking? And, do you really *believe* that you only need to *desire* it and be willing to *accept* it in order to *have* what you want? How much do you believe: "Ask and it will be given to you; seek and you will find; knock and the door will be opened to you" (Matt 7:7)?

The only block to experiencing prosperity is our belief in scarcity. We can look anywhere and see poverty, war, destitution, lack, and a sagging economy, or we can see wealth, prosperity, health, and abundance. What we focus on is our choice. Do you consistently watch the 10 o'clock news and listen to the endless saga of crime, violence, and hatred, or do you watch the learning channel or PBS and soak up new, healthier dimensions of living?

The way of the Tao is "going with the flow," which means that you don't have to effort or struggle, but simply and clearly put out to the universe what you want (your intention) and then patiently wait for the universe to grant it.

Notice where and how you spend your time during the day. How much of your time is devoted to the things you love to do? What you focus on expands, and what you think about, you bring about. Are you doing the things that bring you joy? Create your intention and focus and watch your abundance blossom!

Let Go of Fear and Worry: Go with the Flow and Trust

Ninety percent of what we worry about never occurs. Instead of worrying about what might happen, choose to allow life to take its course. Choice empowers us; resistance causes us to suffer. What we resist persists. Let go of the picture you hold that defines how it should be. Worry, fear, and doubt block your energy, and when your energy is blocked you stop the flow.

Trust allows you to proceed with uncertainty into the unknown. Once you've made a decision, know that the choice you made is exactly as it should be for what you need to learn at this stage of your growth. When things don't go your way, see the opportunity to redirect and refocus. Be open to the wide range of possibilities and ways for things to come to you. Decide to float downstream instead of swimming upstream. What will it take to surrender your idea of how it "should" be for the way it is? How would your life be different if you got out of your own way and trusted that things will work out?

Practice Gratitude

When you give thanks for all the blessings in your life and recognize the perfection in everything, you are opening yourself up to receive more. Being grateful is like the magnet that attracts more good stuff. Instead of complaining about lack and deprivation, be grateful for what is working in your life. Sometimes from your vantage point it may not look too good. Change your view and look at it with a different lens. See what is working and be thankful for all that you do have. And if you are really feeling a lack, be thankful for the things in nature that surround you. We all have plenty to be grateful for. A grateful heart is a full heart.

Living these principles opens the flow and fills my life with abundance daily. By fully appreciating what I have; staying out of worry, fear and doubt; and focusing on what I want and what is working, the channels open so I can receive the plentiful supply of abundance that is already there just for the asking. I believe that the simplest thing we need to do is to set the stage to receive by practicing these principles.

About
Claire Walsh

Claire, a native of New Jersey, moved from the Jersey Shore to the Denver metro area in the early 70's and has found the Colorado climate and spectacular scenery quite favorable for her outdoor interests in biking, golfing, and hiking. She is passionate about maintaining a lifestyle that integrates her personal interests with her desire to encourage others to live their purpose and do it effortlessly.

Blending 20 years expertise in Human Resources in both the public and private sector, with an emphasis in high-tech, Bachelor of Science in Management, and Professional Coach training through Coach University, Claire inspires individuals to discover their passion and live their potential.

As a Personal Life Coach, Claire does what she loves and helps others do the same. She works with employees, managers, career seekers, and individuals in personal, business, and life transitions to help them stretch, grow, and evolve and close the gaps from where they are to where they want to be. Claire loves working with individuals to support them in making changes, especially the internal changes necessary to create the life they want. Her clients develop clarity, focus, and direction and discover ways to live in harmony with their values. She believes everyone has within them the personal power to create the kind of life that will bring true joy and happiness. By tapping into the wisdom within, clients reawaken their spirit and live life more fully and effortlessly.

Claire has demonstrated effectiveness in coaching individuals to achieve greater understanding of themselves, and to make informed decisions for optimal results and greater satisfaction. She is affiliated with Coach University, the International Coach Federation, Coachville, and the Denver Coach Federation.

You can contact Claire by email at clairewalsh@att.net or by calling 303-796-9887.

Maximal Deliciousness

_____

By Nancy Mindes

*"They always say time changes things,
but actually you have to change them yourself. "
~ Andy Warhol*

*"Wealth is when you have the things that money can't buy."
~ Garth Brooks*

Having spent most of my working life in the fast-paced and status symbol-driven fashion industry, I have learned one thing. The one who has the most Prada shoes does not necessarily have the most abundant life. While having a fabulous designer wardrobe, a table at the latest trendy restaurant, fancy vacations, and a loft in Tribeca are great, having all of that does not always mean that happiness will follow. The trick is to be unconditionally delighted with whatever you have, and with some elbow grease and passion, your life will be transformed.

To me, achieving abundance is living life with an attitude of "maximal deliciousness," a phrase I borrowed from The Chow Hound, Jim Leff, who reviews off the beaten path restaurants in New York City on National Public Radio (NPR).

What maximal deliciousness means to me is taking the ordinary and making it extraordinary. Abundance is about delighting, relishing, cherishing, and enjoying the smallest of moments. Abundance is having a willingness to see things as they are, to surrender, let go, and have fun. It is being grateful, joyful, and loving. See your riches and share them with glee. Celebrate life. Be light. Dance your own dance with gusto. Live your life that way and the Prada's will follow.

Although I knew all the rules, the concepts, and platitudes about living abundantly, I often found myself caught up in the daily struggle of wanting more. All too frequently when I would look at what I had, it came up short. I would preach abundance and get stuck in lack.

For example, I would go to a friend's house and find a home finished to perfection. Upon returning home, my eyes could only see the flaws and imperfections and then my envy and dissatisfaction level would begin to rise. Shopping never really fixed the problem because it came from a place deeper than my credit card could take me. I wanted something else.

I used to think there must be someone to blame for this. Maybe it's because my parents divorced when I was a child and money was always tight. For years, I struggled my way through life. The Bare Naked Ladies Song, "If I had a Million Dollars" could have been an anthem for me. I discovered however, that happiness comes from a place inside that has nothing to do with money.

Now don't get me wrong. Having the money to pay for the things you want is much better than not. Yet money, or the lack of it, has frequently kept me stuck in my place. Living my life solely in pursuit of money has not been the best route to getting it. I have recently learned that if you want more money, you must understand your own self-worth, have a financial plan, take a single daily action to move yourself in the direction you want to go, and don't let fear get in your way. Then mix it all together with love and an attitude of gratitude.

Sometimes being grateful doesn't come naturally. Bad habits, weak belief systems, and conditioning can lead one to focus more on the things we don't have than on the things we do. Life's lessons have taught me that if I want to change things, then I need to change my point of view.

I began a gratitude journal when my husband Mark gave me a most treasured gift for Chanukah in 1996, a copy of Sarah Ban Breathnach's timeless book, "Simple Abundance." My gratitude journal is a never-ending source for counting my blessings. Each evening before I go to sleep, I write at least five things, large and small, that I am grateful for. I begin each entry with, I am grateful for… and then I fill it in. Sometimes when the nonsense from the day overtakes me, I simply write, "I am grateful this day is over and I am in my nice comfortable bed. Amen."

And yet, as grateful as I believed I was, there was still a place within where my heart was hard and I was grasping at life instead of savoring the simplest of pleasures with gusto. I still was living with judgments and often came from a place of lack. Somehow, I wasn't really walking my talk.

Losses can be instructive. Recently while listening to a story on NPR on the current crisis in the Catholic Church, a spokesperson was saying how, "Out of suffering, God can bring new life."

That is if you are willing to have new eyes.

The September morning was beautiful as I drove to the train station. Weather-wise, September 11, 2001 was one of the best days of the year. On my car radio Frank DeFord, the sports commentator on WNYC, was pondering the magnitude of Michael Jordan's comeback and it's meaning to the NBA. Just as his story ended, Satirius Johnson, the newscaster for Morning Edition, announced that there had been an accident. A plane had struck the World Trade Center. Was it a small plane that got lost? No, the newscaster on the scene reported it was an American Airlines Boeing 757 jetliner that flew straight into the building. Was the pilot ill?

I boarded an 8:51 Long Island Rail Road train bound for New York City thinking about the horrible accident. As I entered the car, I realized I was the only person who knew because the other passengers were engrossed in their usual morning train rituals. I asked the man in the seat next to me if he worked downtown. Then I told him why.

At Jamaica Station in Queens, a young woman college student got on with a portable radio and just then, the second plane hit the second tower. She spontaneously cried out. Now everyone knew. I could sense the fear and panic. Cell phones came out. Most didn't work. Mine did. I shared it with the man sitting next to me who wanted to call his wife to let her know he was on the train and not in his office near the Trade Center. I was holding my breath and feeling tense.

Was I riding into the gates of hell, I wondered? I felt drawn by a need to be in the city. As the train sped along, I thought about the many happy days my husband, Mark, and I spent under those magnificent Towers. Could they get everyone out and put out the fires? I thought of happier times.

Mark and I met in the summer of 1984. On our first date we went roller-skating at the Roxy roller rink on 18th Street and 10th Avenue, once a hangout for celebrities like Cher. Often after skating, we would drive downtown past the construction site of the World Financial Center and Battery Park City, which was built upon the immense landfill made from the debris excavated to create the great underground city beneath the World Trade Center.

As the months and years went by, it became a city within the city. In 1986, we were married. I quit my job and went back to college, and then went to work as a temporary worker in both the World Trade and World Financial Centers. For 18 months, I watched the unfolding of a neighborhood and enjoyed New York at its most glorious, with new restaurants and store openings and jazz Wednesdays in the Twin Towers Plaza. There were Kodo drum concerts under the palm trees in the Cesar Pelli-designed Winter Garden, Alvin Ailey dance recitals, and Norman Rockwell and Blue Dog Art exhibits.

I took strolls to the marina for lunch, and realized this would be a great place for us to go skating. The area became one of our regular skating spots along the ever-growing paths that begin on the lower West Side at Battery Park City and grow into Hudson River Park. Once, we danced the night away, drank brandy, and smoked cigars in the World's Greatest Bar at Windows on the World. Sometimes in the evenings, we would skate in the World Trade Center Plaza, then lie down on the curved benches of cool cement that encircled the golden ball fountain.

"Can you see the top?" We would ask each other, knowing that was a silly question. Never was there a time when I wasn't amazed by those massive columns of stone and steel piercing the New York sky.

As I sat on the train and watched the smoke coming out of the Towers, I thought of a recent August night. Mark and I skated along the Battery Park City Esplanade and had the place all to our selves. The evening air was still, but cool. At the very tip of the Esplanade stood the Statue of Liberty across the harbor, and when we turned, there above us were those Towers. In the distance, music was playing from one of the yachts in the marina. This was living. I was moved to tears by the pleasure of the memory.

When the train pulled into Pennsylvania Station, I was jolted back into reality. As we spilled onto the platform, I overhead someone say that one of the Towers had collapsed. A plane had crashed into the Pentagon, and another had crashed into a field. No, I thought, this can't be happening.

There I was dressed in my Ferragamo heels and tight fashion-right skirt all set to go to the New York Ready-to-Wear shows at Bryant Park. As you can imagine, I felt more than a bit ridiculous. We were under attack and there I am running around on two-inch heels. Reality was becoming more and more surreal. My mind shifted into overdrive.

I headed toward the tents at 42nd Street just a few blocks from my office. The shows were cancelled and the crowds were letting out. A publicist for one of the designers said to me tearfully, "This must be really bad, the fashion industry never gives up." She spoke the truth. The city was in a state of emergency. Complete lockdown. No one coming in, no one going out. No buses. No subways. I wanted to speak to my husband, a principal in the South Bronx; I needed an anchor.

As I started to run up 5th Avenue to get to my office on 48th, the streets were filled with people staring downtown in disbelief at the scene they were witnessing. From that vantage point the Towers are clearly visible. One was already gone; the other was in grave distress. In the moment I turned to look downtown, the second Tower of the World Trade Center seemed to implode, with debris flying everywhere. It disintegrated and fell straight to the ground, gone in a matter of seconds.

What I saw did not really register. How could the Towers fall like that? My god, I thought, there are thousands of people who work in the Towers. It's the size of a city really. Then I crumbled too, right in the middle of the street in tears. I wondered if the world was coming to an end, and I began to feel ill. I took off my shoes and ran to my office to cry and call my husband. I felt helpless and lost.

Nothing would ever be the same.

On Friday, September 14th, I sat parked in my car and listened to the prayer service broadcast live from the National Cathedral in Washington D.C. and wept. I wondered what it was that brought us here? How could anyone hate with such force that they would destroy thousands of innocent people and sacrifice their own lives? What could I do to change my life? How could I be of service? Would it matter?

Over the weekend, Mark and I took long walks on the beach in the relentlessly beautiful sunshine, taking comfort in the beauty of nature and getting out with others. We listened to the silence. No planes flew overhead. My anger rose when the wind blew and filled my nose with the acrid smell of the fires.

Sunday, September 16, Bette Midler, Oprah Winfrey, Mayor Giuliani, James Earl Jones, and clergy from every religion assembled in Yankee Stadium at a Prayer for America. Mark and I watched the live broadcast at home. Broken-hearted and afraid, I cried a river of tears. I don't think I ever used as many tissues as I did that day. I asked God to forgive me and to save us.

Monday, September 17, Mayor Giuliani encourages everyone to go back to work. As I waited for the 8:51 train, I looked around me. I wanted to notice the people standing there, to look at my neighbors, to see their humanity. Upon arriving at Penn Station, I trembled as I stepped onto the subway platform, yet I felt a new relationship with the people who stood with me. We were in this together. When I got onto the subway and I looked into the eyes of my fellow riders, I could sense the hurt and the sadness. I smiled and was smiled back at with a knowing glance of connection. When I emerged from the subway and stepped onto Fifth Avenue, I discovered I had new eyes. The city I so dearly loved suddenly became all the more precious. As I passed Rockefeller Center, I noticed every nuance of color and line in the architecture, I noticed each person who walked by and silently celebrated them.

On September 18, Rosh Hashanah, the Jewish high holy days that are also known as the Days of Awe, begins. I prayed for Ed and John, family members of people I knew and cared about, who were lost in the Towers. I prayed for the 32 families in my town who had lost loved ones, and I prayed for each person we lost 6000 times. I prayed for the people on the planes, and the Pentagon. I prayed for all of us venturing into our brave new world.

When I looked to my right, I was grateful to see my husband there in the next chair. His presence in my life took on new meaning. I was one of the lucky ones; my life was shaken, but not shattered. I made a decision. I was not going to allow the terrorists to terrorize me. And then our rabbi said the magic words... "Go into the city, spend your money and your time, support them like you never have before." Determined to go ahead with life, I would use the strength of my position as an event producer to bring people together, as well as generate a little financial juice to keep people working. And of course, Mark and I would be going out a little more now too. I got busy making plans to enjoy life, terrorism be damned.

"Live juicy." ~ SARK

On September 26, The Fashion Group International presented a luncheon symposium at the New York Hilton on the state of the retail industry. The luncheon became a multi-level event: a celebration of life, a place to come to hug, to cry, and even share a few smiles. For some, it was their first time venturing out, and many felt very fragile. Being among friends was a tonic. The room was decorated with red, white, and blue bouquets in glass vases surrounded by miniature American flags loaned by the United Services Organization (USO). When I insisted that the show must go on, I had a new appreciation for my position. The opportunity gave me a tool to contribute in some small way. The event brought people together. It helped to keep workers in their jobs. It pumped money into the economy. Without realizing it, I had achieved abundance in a very subtle and powerful way.

Saturday evening, September 29. I have to take several deep breaths to keep from fainting in the car coming in when I see the smoke on the horizon from the underground fires. My anxiety level is a little high. As we walk along the empty Avenue of the Americas, I think that if there are any tourists around they must be hiding. We are on our way to Radio City Music Hall to see Tony Bennett and kd lang perform live. Radio City is an elegant, gilded Art Deco palace and one of the miracles of New York. I cherish that we are able to come and be a part of this evening. We, the audience, are all as one as we submit without complaints to a full body search with a metal detector, a little pat down, and a bag check. My heart races with excitement as I enter the lobby and see the grand staircase and the breath-taking murals. When kd and Tony step on stage, it's magical.

Around the same time, the funerals for the firefighters and police officers begin. The bagpipes play Amazing Grace in their mournful wail each day as they make their way to St. Patrick's Cathedral. I stop to pay my respects as the procession heads for the doors of the great cathedral. The city, once crowded with tourists, is quiet and empty. I often find myself dizzy and overcome when I see this tragic spectacle. On October 3rd, I rush to the emergency room with severe head pains and a fear of dying. I spend the night at Lenox Hill Hospital, and it turns out I am experiencing a post-traumatic stress reaction. The doctor's prescription: burst into tears whenever I feel like it, and a side order of Clonapin to calm my nerves.

I decide to skip the medication and become a serial crier.

On October 8th, I watched the Columbus Day parade from my eighth floor window above 5th Avenue. Firefighters, police, and emergency workers march by to cheers from the crowd. Then something odd: a huge group of people in white sweat shirts came marching down the avenue, waving shopping bags emblazoned with logos like Gucci, Fendi, and Bloomingdale's. As they marched, they waved to the television crews. When they came under my window, I got a better look at their shirts: Oregon loves NY. The Oregonians! I raced downstairs. They were young and old, on foot and on crutches, in wheelchairs and baby carriages. They had flown here to spend their money, send their love, share in our sorrow, and offer support. Hooray... in my gratitude journal that night, my entry read, "I am grateful for the Oregonians." I made a mental note to go to Oregon to return the favor.

The following day, as I came up out of the subway, the bagpipes were playing. Thousands of firefighters and policemen lined 5th Avenue. The traffic was stopped as the procession of limousines and the horse drawn casket made its way to St. Patrick's. It was such a beautiful morning. I made my way down the street with an intention to stop at the Cathedral to pay my respects. I started to stagger and sob uncontrollably. Somewhere, as I stumbled along, I felt a hand reach out and an arm pull me in. When I looked up, there was a man as big as a tree wearing a button on his plaid shirt and it read, "Oregon loves NY." He said, "I am so sorry for your pain." And he began to cry.

"LIVE AS THOUGH HEAVEN IS ON EARTH." ~ UNKNOWN

For one brief moment of connection my life changed yet again. On that day and every day since, I have found myself savoring the delights of my life all the more. My appreciation for the simplest of pleasures that began on the worst September morning in history continues to blossom.

Jealousies and judgments fade into love and appreciation faster. Petty squabbles and silly arguments quickly turn into laughter and good times, because life is too much fun to waste it on playing small.

As I see my life today, I know it is already rich and abundant. And just by recognizing that my life is perfect and oh so grand, I have attracted new people and new opportunities by being present to the truth of the splendor and joy in my life. Each day I look forward to the routine and the surprises that come my way.

On September 26th, I wrote in my journal, "Since the World Trade Center attack, I have been reconsidering my life and my attitude toward everyone. Once, I believed I was kind and grateful, loving, gentle, and strong. The truth is, I had the capacity yet not the reality. With a constant edge of anger and a lingering list of hurts, I wasn't able to be who I thought I was. As a New Yorker, I will always have a snap, crackle, and pop, yet today I know I have new eyes. And, I hope, a more open heart. At my core is a sense of a deepening spirituality, a pull from the universe to serve in some way, and a desire for lightness, for seeing that the only catastrophes in my life are self-created, how I choose to view the world."

"ENJOY YOURSELF, IT'S LATER THAN YOU THINK." ~ THE SPECIALS

My new view starts by being grateful, counting blessings, and savoring moments. Tasting my food and enjoying the flavors, the textures, and the love that went into preparing it. I appreciate how fragile our lives are and relish the incredible gift of living another day.

On October 24 at a gala I planned honoring celebrity families, I got to meet Bette Midler and thank her with a hug and a kiss for singing her song, "Wind Beneath My Wings" at the Prayer for America. She loved my outfit and wanted to know where I got my lace pants. For me, this was maximal deliciousness in action.

Mark and I continued to go out and be a part of it—New York, New York.

One balmy night in October after a dance recital at the Brooklyn Academy of Music, we went to the promenade in Brooklyn Heights, just below the Brooklyn Bridge. Once, it was the place to see one of the best views of the Twin Towers and the amazing New York skyline. The candle shrines had long since burned out and their remnants remained. The smell of the underground fires permeated the air. The smoke gave it an eerie haze. I pulled my soft cashmere shawl around me for comfort as I read the letters, cards, and prayers interspersed with the photos of the missing attached to the wrought iron fences. I wept for what was lost. And, as I looked again at what wasn't there, I saw too what was. That in our loss we still were standing and going on. And the wondrous skyline that is New York was still an awe-inspiring sight.

On October 27th, Mark and I celebrated our 15th Wedding Anniversary. It was a strange weather day, raw-cold and very windy. Still, we had a plan to be outdoors. As an anniversary gift, Mark bought me a Robert Rauschenberg print of the Statue of Liberty holding the Twin Towers in her left arm. Three words are emblazoned across the bottom: **I Love NY**.

We put on our skates and headed down Hudson River Park to get as close as we could to our favorite skating spot, closed because it is at Ground Zero. My intention was to say goodbye to all that was, to pray for what can be, to pay tribute, and to celebrate the joy of the life we have together.

The wind blew us down in a flash, and as we drew closer to Ground Zero, the atmosphere and the energy began to change. To describe the scene would be impossible. As I stood there, I was waiting for Steven Spielberg to yell, "cut" and then the set would be dismantled. We lingered a while. The scene was real to me now. Then it was time to go.

As we turned up Maiden Lane, there was a whirring sound from the street sweeper's endless task to clean away the concrete dust. The klieg lights from Ground Zero threw an eerie pall on the scene. I spotted Richard Dreyfuss standing in the glow of a street lamp with a priest and a nurse. A perpetual eavesdropper, I overheard them talking about the preparations for the memorial service planned for the next day at the site. Thankfully, I would not be among those who would be invited.

"THE REAL VOYAGE OF DISCOVERY CONSISTS NOT IN SEEKING NEW LANDSCAPES, BUT IN HAVING NEW EYES." ~ MARCEL PROUST

Recently, when I asked a client what he was grateful for, he went silent. He had no idea at all. I asked if he would be willing to keep a gratitude journal. After much hemming and hawing, he decided this was something he could do. I made no promises of riches or fame. However, when he began keeping one, his point of view and his life began to change. The job he hated improved. His non-existent love life began to pick up dramatically. He started attracting new people and friends into his life. Most of all he was able to really see, maybe for the first time, the richness and texture of his life. He told me that once he started writing in his gratitude journal, he just couldn't stop. And, an unexpected bonus was the fun and pleasure he had doing the daily noticing of the wonderfulness of his life.

What about you? What will it take for you to achieve abundance? What if you start by going for maximal deliciousness? Find out what you value most, and then orient your life around your values as your guiding star. I ask you not to wait a moment longer. Be playful, seek out the sublime in the ordinary, celebrate the small, have a light heart, bless mother earth, connect with spirit, seek stillness, awaken your senses, and cherish every moment.

About
Nancy Mindes

Nancy Mindes is a Coach University-trained Professional Life Coach and founder of NYWoman.com, a soon-to-be launched web center for women who want to create a life of Joy, Passion, and Purpose.

Known as " The Inner-Style Coach," Nancy works with creative entrepreneurial women and men who seek to effortlessly integrate their personal and professional selves so that they can have the life of their wildest imagining. She has a unique ability "to see past the words" and "hear the feeling" that gives her clients permission to speak their truth and take positive action. She possesses the wisdom of maturity and experience, coupled with the lightness and playfulness of youth.

A sought-after professional speaker and group coaching leader, Nancy has created a fun and interactive program, *Relax and Release Your Inner Beauty*™, which is frequently a spark that ignites and catalyzes participants to seek exciting inner adventures that can propel them to new heights.

Nancy writes a column entitled "Xtreme Self Care," which appears regularly in The Fashion Group International Global Bulletin and periodically on their website, www.fgi.org, she is also their event producer-coach. She is the creator of Unmistakably Arden, a concept for organizational change she developed for Elizabeth Arden.

Nancy is a founding member of Coachville, a member of The International Coach Federation, and is an officer of Toastmasters International.

Ms. Mindes lives in Rockville Centre, Long Island, New York. To contact her, call 516-764-1748 or email her at Nancy@NYWoman.com. Her web business card is www.NancyMindes.com

The Journey of Abundance

By Jordana Tiger

Jerry had spent the day fishing at a beautiful lake in the mountains with his good buddy Frank. Following fishing etiquette, they had sat in silence most of the day, bonding as they enjoyed the beauty of nature and their time at a favorite activity. Yet with all of the abundance surrounding him, Jerry felt frustrated because he hadn't caught the number of fish he had hoped to catch. When he told me of his frustration during a coaching call, I suggested that he share with me the most important thing he had gotten out of his day with Frank. Was it truly the number of fish he caught, or was it the time he had spent with a good friend in a place of tranquility? Was his view of abundance driven by a need for quantity, not quality? Was catching more fish really going to make the experience better?

Jerry began to see that the quality of the time with his friend was what made the day enjoyable. He began to see that when he viewed his experiences from the inside out—instead of what he "got" in a material way—that he could enjoy the time no matter the outcome.

Defining abundance is a difficult task. People have a different view of what it means to them. Some immediately associate it with money or the quantity and type of "things" they accumulate. But I believe that is a limited view.

A simple definition of abundance is finding complete happiness and a feeling of peace within. Building further on that definition, abundance can mean having self-esteem, self-respect, satisfying and fulfilling relationships with your family and friends, and good health. Abundance can also mean playing full out and enjoying *all* the moments in life, not just an end result. Abundance is the feeling I get when I'm sitting by a campfire: peaceful and full of quality and healing. Just a tent, the stars, and time with a friend or a loved one.

For me, abundance is also about the process. It's about the quality, not the quantity; it's about one's spiritual and emotional health, not materialism. Abundance is enjoying the journey of life and learning lessons as they occur, of being in the present. For example, if I'm studying for an exam, what I'm learning is more important than the grade I receive. If I'm going to the movies with a friend, the time together is more important than the movie. When I disagree with someone, what's important is the way we work it out, not the actual problem. Spending quality time with others and being present with my feelings at that moment—that's abundance!

Achieving abundance is a life-long process, a journey that requires you to explore deep into your soul. And it's a path that is worth the work. My hope is that this chapter will expand your view of what abundance is, and how you can bring it into your life in a lasting, loving way.

Abundance Is An Inside Job

To achieve a feeling of abundance, you must be whole and complete within. When you feel good about yourself, you will treat yourself with dignity, taking care to bring those things into your life that offer a sense of abundance. You will spend the rest of your life with yourself. You might as well make it worthwhile by being healthy in all aspects of life: emotionally, mentally, physically, and spiritually. As each of these parts become stronger within yourself, you will thrive and flourish in your relationships with others. Once you are on the road to the best "you" possible, you are also on the road to yet a better one with someone else. While the journey is challenging, it is also meaningful. Let's take a look at how to start making those "inside" changes.

First of all, you must start with a baseline of where you are now. I find this process helpful to see where you start, so you know where to go. There are many ways to do this, so I will explain the way I believe works tremendously well with my clients. Assess all areas of your life by rating yourself on a scale from 1-10 with 10 being the highest level of satisfaction (how happy or abundant) you feel in each of the categories. Here are examples of categories, but by all means, you can also make up those that fit your life. These are some I use with my clients: Health, Career, Significant Other Relationship, Friends, Family, Money, Fun and Recreation, Spiritual Growth, Personal Growth, and Physical Environment. Attach numbers to each of these categories. You can then see if your life is also in balance. Are your numbers low or high? Is there a variety? What is missing in your life in each area? What would give you a greater sense of abundance? What must happen in your life for the numbers to all reach a "10"? What do you need to get there? This is where the goal setting process starts. Of course, each one of you might define abundance differently for yourself. So this is a good place for you to start looking at what abundance means to you personally. Abundance for you can be wealth, feeling a high level of self-esteem, feeling fullness and love in life, feeling competent and sufficient, or having plenty of "something." For me, I like to think of it as how I feel inside about myself, and also whether I am following my heart, my soul, and living out my dreams and passions. What will it be for you?

Thoughts are Powerful

I believe that thoughts are powerful. Ernest Holmes says that abundance belongs to everyone, yet not everyone uses that principle or has that belief. Emmet Fox also believes that you can have abundance no matter what your circumstances are. I believe your attitude and faith can help lead you to feeling abundant in life. We only lack in the world if we *think* we lack. Feeling abundance is completely loving and enjoying what we already have in life; it's honoring what already exists.

I have a friend who feels completely abundant with the love from her family. During the holidays, many people give huge gifts with a large sum of money attached to them. However, my friend comes from a very poor family and all through childhood felt the struggle her parents went through to make ends meet. Their Christmas gifts were full of love rather than full of "money." Her three brothers and sisters and parents hand-made most of their gifts or gave gifts such as painting a picture, baking cookies, or giving a few pair of socks to each of her family members. Most of society would think that those were small gifts, but they were given with the utmost amount of love in their hearts. That was all they could afford, yet if you looked at them interacting with others, at work, at home, and with their friends, you would never suspect they didn't have money. My friend is always happy, grateful, and giving of herself. Most of our friends assume she has money because of how abundant she feels. She describes herself as feeling grateful, content, and full of everything she ever wanted. She rarely complains about anything and walks around with complete confidence. She is someone who everyone loves, and unless you know the details of her life, would never think she came from an extremely poor family. She feels abundant and chooses to think and act that way in all areas of her life. Her abundance is about love. Again, I'm asking you, what is it for you?

We can choose to think we are abundant or we can choose to think we lack many things. One thing we know is that we can't change what other people think of us, but we have control over what we think about ourselves and how we use thought in general. How we think about ourselves and our world helps us to actually step up to the plate and live that way. If we know we are abundant in the world, we will feel it, and it will be part of our existence.

Attitude Affects Abundance

Your attitude and outlook on life, as well as your perspective, are all key issues in becoming whole and complete within. Sometimes we encounter difficult situations. How you look at the issues behind the situation and the meaning you attach to those issues will impact the outcome. While you may not have a choice about what actually happened, you have a powerful choice about how you approach the facts. You also may not necessarily have a choice about how you feel. Yet you can choose what response you will have to those feelings. This is a hard concept for many people to grasp. And it is one of the most important concepts to allow you to move forward and to keep you from the baggage of your past, to keep you in a place of forgiveness, and to allow you to have a big life instead of a small one.

Let me give you an example. Most people awake each morning to an alarm clock. Many people continue to press the snooze button, getting up slowly, and agonizing over the day. However, you have a choice to continue pressing the snooze or you have the choice to get up with energy and say, "I'm going to make this my best day ever." You will find that the day you jump out of bed and *choose* the attitude of having a great day, your day will not only be better, it will contain more fulfillment and contentment than if you had chosen the "what a drag" attitude. Try this positive attitude for a week and you will begin to see an internal shift that lasts. You will begin to see a day at a time how powerful your choices can be.

Now let's take a more difficult example. I have a client, Paula, whose husband left her for another woman. Paula grieved her relationship, yet felt that the grief was going on too long. After being depressed for months, she eventually was willing to try my suggestion of some perspective work. She no longer wanted that attitude and heavy weight on her.

I suggested she use a pie chart to give her the freedom to make each piece of the pie represent the attitude she wanted to take. I asked her to make up some ways she could "choose to be" in this situation. Some of her choices were: to be depressed, laugh about it, be grumpy, forgive and move on, be dramatic, be happy to get rid of him and move on to someone better, learn and grow with peace and love, or be resentful. In doing this activity, she was able to see that she could choose any of the eight attitudes she wrote down. This method gave her a powerful way to look at her choices.

There is a time to grieve when you lose a relationship. Yet so many people stay in that place. With my encouragement, Paula decided to try on a new attitude and see if it could help her. She chose to "learn and grow with peace and love." Within a few weeks, she was back to her old self, taking yoga classes, dance classes, and even starting to go out with friends again to possibly meet someone new. She could have chosen to stay in that place of grief. That was always a choice. My coaching helped her to see other options and other perspectives. I assisted her in owning her power of choice. She realized how meaningful this exercise was for her and now uses it with all of her decision-making.

My suggestion to you is to be proactive and take charge of your attitude. This exercise can work with any situation you have where you need to make a decision, or if you are feeling stuck in a situation. You have the power to choose your attitude. Why focus on the negative when you can choose the positive or choose a brand new perspective you have never considered before? What a powerful concept! Understanding this concept is an important step on the journey to abundance.

Living with Gratitude

Having a sense of gratitude also leads to having a sense of abundance. Be grateful and appreciate all the wonderful things and people in your life. The grass is not always greener on the other side. Most people don't even realize until something traumatic happens in their life that they had some absolutely wonderful moments and let them go to waste.

Keeping a gratitude list can often help. A gratitude list is a tool that can remind you of all the things you have. And

I'm not referring to material things. This is the time to write down and list all the terrific people you have surrounding you and the fortunate things you have that make you feel safe and secure. Look at the little things. Those are often forgotten until it is too late. Don't let that happen to you.

For example, write down that you had a great conversation with someone at work, a wonderful workout at the gym, a postcard from a vacationing friend. Look back at your day and think of all the things that you usually take for granted and write those down. If you do this every night, you will start to feel more abundant. I suggest this tool because it helps you shift your attitude to a more abundant consciousness and brings positive thinking to your heart. When you can choose your thoughts and begin to believe you have emotional and peaceful abundance in your life, you have succeeded in a journey many never attempt. I encourage you to practice positive thinking, practice feeling love and gratitude, and I truly believe you will begin to feel abundance inside your soul.

Abundant Qualities

When you have abundant qualities such as compassion, sincerity, generosity, and unconditional love in your soul, then you also have reason to feel abundant. You feel good about yourself when you have tapped into these qualities. When you feel good about yourself, you tend not to have a poverty consciousness; instead you have an abundant one, with regards to love and peace, quality, and meaning in your life. When you feel this amazing energy, you feel amazing abundance.

I have a friend who has breast cancer. However, she is a very positive woman who treats everyone with the utmost respect and love. She always asks how someone is doing, always has a smile on her face, and is definitely always ready to tell a joke and share a funny story. My friend will also share with others her viewpoint on how life is too short to have a negative attitude. She brings love to others by her compassion for people, sincerity and generosity with others, and by having unconditional love for everyone she meets. She is definitely full of abundance no matter what her health situation brings. Even after days of chemotherapy and radiation, she will reach out and share love. Sure, she often feels ill, yet her love of people shines through and everyone she touches can feel her abundant thinking and love. She feels good about who she is and even though she is sick, she tells us all that she feels peace and love in her life. She is an amazing inspiration to all who know her.

Yet, there are many people who stay stuck in a poverty consciousness, which is thinking the worst about everything and thinking negative about what they have. I have a client who came to me with this type of thinking. She didn't have money growing up. She was in several relationships that ended with much anger and resentment. She then continued to live with anger and resentment in her heart and soul, as well as her everyday living. She complained constantly about everything that happened to her throughout the day, only being able to see the negative. There were some good and bad things that happened to her throughout the day. However, my point is that she ONLY saw the negative. She looked at life through the viewpoint of "less than" and "lack of…".

This is an example of looking at life through a poverty consciousness. Thinking everything will turn out sour in your life; thinking that just because you had a bad relationship that you will have another one. Poverty consciousness is continuing any negative thought, continuing any negative situation in your mind. I worked with her for months on her thought process. I continually encouraged her to create a set of affirmations that focused on positive things. She had a very difficult time thinking that anything good could come of her situation or her life. Getting her to do affirmations (positive thoughts) was difficult. She resisted most of the time. However, she did finally start to write and say positive affirmations aloud every day. An example of what she said was, "I create and have loving relationships with others." "I feel love in my heart." She said these affirmations every day for months and reports to me that she has opened up her thinking to allow others to come into her life. She has been dating someone for a few months now and is seeing that she is lovable. This is just one simple example of how you have a choice over your thinking. My client still has work to do, and we continue to work on changing her negative thinking into positive abundant thinking.

The next story is another example of changing a poverty consciousness into an abundant one. I have a client who worked in a job for the state. She made a lot of money doing something she absolutely disliked. However, she was caught in the trap many people find themselves in, and that is working in a job they don't like, but think they can't get out of because of the money. (Or choose to stay because of the money.) She felt trapped in this job, felt negative about going to work, and was thinking she would always stay in the frustration of making ends meet. She struggled financially even with her high paying job and she was so depressed that she was struggling with maintaining her friendships as well. One day, she came to me and told me she was going to quit her job to take up another job that paid less than half of what she was making because it involved something she absolutely loved. She was so excited, and I could definitely see the spark in her eye. She quit her job on the spot and started in the new job. She, of course, was struggling financially for awhile. However, something amazing happened to her over the next six months. Her face was bright, her eyes were sparkling, her mood was always positive and happy, and she was feeling complete joy in her new life. Over the next year, she ended up making just as much money and was feeling such abundance in her life for all the friends and love she had in life. She went from feeling depressed with her poverty consciousness into feeling happiness with her abundant consciousness. She was doing something she absolutely loved and it made a huge difference in her attitude in every area of her life. She has amazing energy and is able to tap into being generous, loving, and kind to everyone. This has made a huge difference in her world.

Love, Integrity, and Happiness

Many people feel material things make one abundant. By now, you can see that is not my way of thinking. What makes you happy? If you are happy, following your true desires, and doing things you love, you have abundance. If you are in a rich and satisfying relationship, you have abundance. If you live a life of "integrity," you have abundance. Material things are good for some things, but abundance is an entity all by itself. Having abundance is a state of mind, not a state of ownership. Abundance is feeling loved, living a life you are proud of, and feeling happiness along the way. I suggest everyone take a look at the bigger picture in their life instead of the tiny details that get in the way and distract us from the truth that life is truly what you make of it, and how you choose to view it.

Obstacles to Abundance

There are many obstacles to abundance: negative thinking, being in a "victim" stance, feeling "less than," worry, and holding on to resentments. All these things will get in the way of feeling abundant.

Negative thinking is usually the most significant reason for feeling a lack of abundance in your life. To change your thinking, you must first be aware of it. You must be connected to what your thoughts are, as well as your emotions. Once you recognize what you are thinking about in a particular situation about yourself, or about a possible action, you then have a choice to continue that thinking or change it. If it is negative, you can stop yourself in the moment and switch your thoughts. This is called "Thought Stopping." Literally, say "Stop" out loud to yourself in the moment you are thinking something negative and replace that thought with a positive one. This takes some practice and work to do, but with time, the new, positive thoughts become automatic and you will begin to see amazing results.

Being in a victim stance will also keep us in the place of "lack" and feeling "less than." Again, stop that thought, replace it with a more positive image of yourself and your situation, and you can make a shift from a victim stance to a more helpful attitude that will lead to abundance.

If you feel "less than," you also have a greater tendency to manipulate or push others around. Again, this will lead to the feeling of lack and having less in life. Also, if you don't like or accept yourself, you will not feel abundant. Sometimes you might not "like" who you are, but if you can accept all that you are, you will not feel a lack consciousness. Once we make peace with ourselves, stay in "integrity" with ourselves, we then have more of us to be proud of, and therefore, have a greater feeling of abundance. Remember, abundance is feeling whole with our self, having a feeling of goodness about our internal selves, and having a feeling of happiness and joy within. If you focus on working with positive thoughts about yourself, despite the "lack" programming you are accustomed to, you will feel you have more in life.

Worrying does nothing but make you worry more. If something bad is going to happen, it will happen anyway. If you spend all your emotional energy worrying about stuff, then you have less energy to work on your abundant thinking. And most likely that negative thing will occur anyway, because as I stated earlier, your thoughts have a lot of control over what actually happens. The more abundant way to think is to live in the moment and think positive things about your situation or find ways to adapt to your situation, even if it may have cause for concern.

Holding on to the past and holding on to resentments will also get in the way of feeling abundant. You cannot change what has already occurred. Let go of your attachment to being right, and to material things as well. Once you release old baggage, you are then free to be in the here and now and that will bring you joy. Resentments block the sunlight from your life. Choose to move forward and abundance will follow. There is a limitless world out there for us if we choose to see it and live in its light.

Summary

Abundance can be many things to many people. Ultimately, having abundance is an ongoing process, a lifelong journey, a path to follow. What I believe works best is for you to figure out what abundance means to you deep in your heart and soul. Only then will the application of the concept of changing your thoughts work in your best interest. Remember, abundance is an inside job, attitude affects abundance, thoughts and choice are powerful, and living with gratitude will help you on the road to abundance. If you possess qualities of love, integrity, and happiness in your heart, you will also have achieved abundance. You can have an awesome life if you choose to follow the steps toward abundance. Your life is worth everything. This is a golden opportunity and my wish is for you to jump on the road to abundant living, now. Put your best foot forward, reach for the best you can be, and may abundant thinking be the choice you make.

About
Jordana Tiger

Jordana Tiger, M.A., M.F.T., Certified Professional Co-Active Coach (C.P.C.C.), is an award-winning public speaker and founder of Awesome Life Coaching, a company specializing in personal development and success. She is a Certified Life Coach who assists others to achieve complete fulfillment in their lives.

Jordana's personal coaching helps to unlock the door for you in regards to your passion and purpose in life. She will help you clarify your values and assist you to see that choice is a powerful word and in your reach. She helps you find balance so you have a life of quality, and she gets you to see you can change obstacles into limitless possibilities. Jordana works with you in being authentic with yourself; therefore, tapping into your own amazing power. She inspires and motivates you to be completely unstoppable in your transformation and commitment to having an awesome life. Jordana can help you increase your overall personal effectiveness and satisfaction, help you set a structure for organization, and keep you accountable for what you say you are up to in life. She will hold you bigger than you at times hold yourself. She will believe in you and keep you headed in a forward direction.

Jordana has coached athletes in the past and now coaches individuals looking for a positive change and greater freedom and success. She works with educators, small business owners, new coaches, and individuals that feel "stuck" and are going through some type of transition in their life. She also works with many individuals who have Attention Deficit Disorder. In her psychotherapy practice she works with individuals on many issues such as addiction/recovery issues, adults who were abused as children, communication between couples, families of special needs children, and HIV/AIDS issues.

Jordana presents workshops and lectures on many topics including life balance, values, and achieving self-esteem through living an authentic life.

Jordana is also a State Credentialed Teacher who works with special needs children, as well as their families. She is a member of the International Coach Federation, Professional Mentors Coaches Association, California Association of Marriage and Family Therapists, Toastmasters International, Business Alliance of Los Angeles, and California Association of Physical Education, Health, Recreation, and Dance.

Jordana is a contributing author of *A Guide to Getting It: Self-Esteem.*

To reach Jordana, call her at (818) 558-9162, email her at JT@AwesomeLifeCoaching.com, or visit her website at www.AwesomeLifeCoaching.com.

The Nature of Abundance and the Art of Living

By Schuyler Morgan

"NATURE IS MAN'S TEACHER. SHE UNFOLDS HER TREASURES TO HIS SEARCH, UNSEALS HIS EYE, ILLUMES HIS MIND, AND PURIFIES HIS HEART; AND INFLUENCE BREATHES FROM ALL THE SIGHTS AND SOUNDS OF HER EXISTENCE." ~ ALFRED BILLINGS STREET

Copia, the Goddess of Abundance, kneels at the water's edge, her hand gently nurturing a young vine. Through her beauty and her kneeling posture, she demonstrates her respect for nature. This goddess represents the link between the symbolic waters of life and a sense of abundance: fullness, endless supply, and an ability to give back. Just as Copia nurtures the vine in her grasp, so must we consider the challenges and possibilities that we encounter as we weave together all that comes our way.

"COME FORTH INTO THE LIGHT OF THINGS, LET NATURE BE OUR TEACHER."
~ WILLIAM WORDSWORTH

The best tutor in the principles of abundance is nature. Her messages are powerful, practical, and immediately applicable. Through those messages, I found the cornerstone of my creative vision: how to make my life my art and my art my life. That understanding has allowed me to reign as a goddess of abundance in my personal realm, which is brimming with possibilities.

Early in my life, I came across the words of John Muir, father of our national parks and founder of the Sierra Club: "I used to envy the father of our race, dwelling as he did among the new made plants and fields of Eden. But I do so no more, for I have discovered that I also live in 'creation's dawn.' The morning stars still sing together, and the world not yet half made, becomes more beautiful every day."

Much as I loved nature, my vision of wilderness seemed nowhere near that ecstatic. I thought, "John, you are either the master of hyperbole or something is going on out there that I need to find out about." So I went into the mountains to live and to explore all the wonders for myself.

The first thing I discovered was that my eyes were clouded, and that nature and life really were just as beautiful as Muir had described, if I was open enough to see.

The second thing I discovered was Muir! Here was a man who walked into nature, saw its beauty and let it fill him up. His life overflowed and that fullness came out in everything he did—in the way he hiked the mountains, in his political activism, in his writing, in his huge Agri-business in Martinez, California. The fullness came out in his life, his voice, and his character.

Muir was a man who made his life his art, and that was a staggering concept for me. Like many, I had been raised in a school system that taught me from the time I was about knee high that there were two things: there was life…and there was art. And they were not the same.

Art was the ultimate elective. Art was what you got to do after everything else was done. Art was creative, art was fun.

Then there was life. Life was serious. Life was hard. You were supposed to do life all the time. And those doing art? Well, they were a little suspect anyway.

What a terrible definition! I believe it kept most of us from ever thinking that we could be creative. Creativity had to do with art, and art had to do with painting and sculpture, and if you didn't do those things you weren't creative.

Muir showed me this wasn't true; that my creativity could come out in everything—in great photographs, in good business decisions, in the way I treated my family, in the service I gave to my community. My creativity could come out in my life. So nature taught Muir and Muir taught me, and "making my life my art" became my life's vision.

"I AM AN ARTIST AT LIVING – MY WORK OF ART IS MY LIFE."
~ SUZUKI

From the time I first picked up a camera, I have celebrated nature through my lens. And nature has responded by teaching me some extraordinary lessons.

The lessons are all around us. Seeing is the challenge. The lessons are also within us, for we, too, are part of nature. Although most of us find it wonderfully refreshing to "get out in nature" and regret the time when we have to go back to the "real" world, the truth is that the "real" world is the world of nature. There are fundamental natural laws or principles that clearly manifest in nature, and wherever we are, we live with the consequences of those laws, whether we recognize it or not.

For many years, I lived in the beautiful Northern California Santa Cruz Mountains and held many events, parties, leadership seminars, and trail rides in a variety of settings, most frequently at my home at Sky Ridge Ranch. To those who attended, I made what I've come to call the "Sky Ridge Promise." If you open yourself to the natural environment, the people and animals around you, and the timeless fundamentals of nature, you will find personal and specific answers to the challenges and opportunities you face on the road to abundance, with it's many tempting detours along the way.

Now I want to assure you that you don't need to come to Sky Ridge Ranch or any place in particular to claim the Sky Ridge Promise. All you have to know is to learn from nature. Every living thing, whether it's a plant, an animal, or an insect, has its own natural habitat. And if it wants to be healthy and normal, it has to live within that environment.

I believe that almost all of my creative ideas have come when I was in tune with nature, where I was emotionally and psychologically in a garden. I have people say to me, "Yeah, but I live in the city. Where can I go to get these experiences?" You don't have to climb Mount Everest; you don't have to be at Big Sur. You can find tranquility in a quiet place when the moon is full and it shines on your face. There is an ecological, theological, and biological reality: the more we are in tune with eternal nature, the more we will be able to hear the still small voice within and have explosions of inspirational insight.

The Three Constants:
Change, Changelessness, and Choice

The key to being in tune with nature is to be open, to really see what it is we're a part of. As we become truly open, we discover that the essence of our pursuit for abundance is dealing effectively with the three constants in our lives: Change, Changelessness, and Choice.

Change

Change is constant, complex, and often rapid. We can't control it. When we try, it becomes frightening, threatening. But we can learn to understand it, to work in harmony with it, to influence it, to cultivate it, to "go with the flow." A coaching client clearly captures the essence of this important point in the following story:

"For six days, we had been running the Colorado River through the Grand Canyon in wooden dories. Besides the crew, there were 18 guests on the trip, all participants in a seminar I was leading.

"Perhaps it had been unfair to tell the participants I would be 'leading' the trip. After floating for nearly a week, they knew that neither the crew nor I was really in control. The river was in charge. We followed its flow.

"I asked the group to think about what it meant to go with the flow?

" 'Going with the flow has taken on a whole new meaning for me down here,' one woman said. 'It doesn't mean turning off your brain; in fact, it's quite the opposite. It means being totally conscious, paying complete attention. For the boatman to survive a rapid, he must first realize that he's riding on a river over which he has little if any, control. If he believes he's the one directing things, he's doomed.'

" 'Going with the flow also means knowing your own boat,' offered another participant, 'Knowing everything it will and won't do, knowing its flip lines and first aid kit, making it an extension of yourself. If you don't know your boat, you'll never make it down the river.'

" 'When I think of going with the flow,' a third participant mused, 'I am not on the river, I am the river—in touch with the source, straining at my borders, full of energy and serenity, ever changing, yet always the same.'

"For ten days the river teaches us its lessons…or maybe the river just is and we take what we need. In either case, when we finally return to the canyon's rim, what we have learned seems to glow not only from each photograph we have taken but from each of us as well."

Nature teaches that change is a vital part of life. Seeds change. Seasons change. Weather changes. People change. We are part of a dynamic, growing environment. Through change, we create better organizations, more productive teams, more harmonious families, and better selves.

The problem comes when we try to create change as though we live in a static environment. We try to fix people, install programs, or repair relationships as though they were isolated, broken parts in some mechanical whole.

But the whole—the business, the community, the family, and the individual—is a complex, highly interrelated ecological system. Each part has a living attachment to every other part. Change in any part affects all parts. When we learn to see daily problems in terms of living systems, it dramatically changes the way we deal with them.

To effectively work with change, we do not always need to understand it, but we do need to respect it. A farmer may not understand every biochemical reaction that causes something to grow, but the more he understands the natural processes of planting, nurturing, and growth, the more productive he becomes.

For the person seeking abundance in their life, change is a friend, a companion, a powerful tool, and the basis of growth. Creating positive change is what abundance is about.

"WHAT THE CATERPILLAR CALLS THE END OF THE WORLD, THE MASTER CALLS A BUTTERFLY" ~ RICHARD BACH

Changelessness

We don't control change, principles do. Nature teaches that there is order in complexity. There are patterns in change. There are natural laws that are in control.

Tides change, but there are principles or dynamics upon which they change. Seeds change, but principles of growth govern their development into mature plants that bear flowers and food.

Depending on the atmosphere, the weather, and the temperature, there's a different sunset every day—but there's always a sunset.

At the very heart of nature are principles that apply everywhere—including our own lives, relationships, and organizations—because we are a part of nature. So we learn from nature that the key to dealing with change is to have a changeless core. A changeless core is to understand, trust, and live in harmony with the natural laws that govern all of life. It's being realistic, living in the present, and having a solid foundation so that change becomes beneficial instead of harmful. Having a changeless core is what produces inner peace, with some degree of predictability, even in the midst of a complex, chaotic environment.

For example, the laws of nature tell you it's ludicrous to think you can goof off all spring, play all summer, throw a bunch of seeds in the ground at the beginning of fall, and reap a bountiful harvest two weeks later. They also tell you there's no way you're going to neglect planning and preparation, avoid building relationships, side-step problems, and end up with a strong, effective self, family, or organization, enjoying the pleasures of abundance.

The laws also tell you that whatever you sow, you're going to reap. If you sow seeds of mistrust through dishonesty, backbiting, using people, or playing political games, you're never going to reap the benefits of a high trust life in the long run. You may experience some apparent short-term results, but they will never endure. In the long term, the laws of nature will govern. In other words, if you plant weeds, you're never going to enjoy a flower garden. The following story by Arun Gandhi, grandson of Mahatma Gandhi, and Founder and President of the M.K. Gandhi Institute for Nonviolence explains this well.

"In my early childhood in South Africa, I worked on the first farm community my grandfather started. At the time, it didn't make much sense to me, and it was hard for me to get up so early in the morning and work. But that experience taught me many valuable lessons.

"I remember my parents and grandparents telling me, 'When you plant the seeds and nurture them, they grow into healthy plants and give you fruit. They multiply. Soon you have a larger patch of whatever you want to grow.' They said that, in the same way seeds multiply when they interact with the elements of nature, our feelings and philosophies also multiply. To make the lesson more understandable, my grandfather would tell me this story:

" 'An ancient king, curious to know about peace and non-violence, asked all the wise people in his kingdom to give him advice on the topic. All tried to explain as best they could, but none could satisfy his curiosity.

" 'Eventually, he was told that there was a wise man who lived at the edge of town, but he would not come to the king. The king would have to go to him if he wanted an answer. So the king went.

" 'After listening to the king's question, the wise man went to the back of his house and came back with a grain of wheat, which he gave to the king. Now, the king was too proud to ask what this meant, so he brought the wheat back to his palace. Knowing that it must be valuable, he put it into a gold box and locked it in his safe. Every day he would open the box and look at the grain of wheat. But nothing ever happened to it, and the king became more and more puzzled.

" 'Eventually another wise man came from out of town and visited the king. The king asked him, 'What does this grain of wheat have to do with peace and nonviolence?' The wise man replied, 'As long as you keep this grain of wheat in a box, locked in your safe, nothing is going to happen to it. It will eventually rot, and there will be nothing left. But if you were to put it in soil and allow it to interact with nature and the elements, it would grow and multiply. Soon you would have a whole field of wheat.'

" 'In the same way, you can't keep peace and non-violence locked up in your heart and mind. You have to allow them to interact with nature and the elements. Then they will grow and multiply.'

"I learned the lesson my grandfather wanted to teach with that story. I also learned more. My garden taught me about being a good friend and a good relative. It taught me how you have to nurture relationships. It also taught me that in order to enjoy the fruits of life, you must work. The work is hard. Sometimes it is difficult to see progress. But seeds do grow and bear fruit.

"I think that working in the garden, and associating that experience so closely with my education and philosophy, has helped me to understand and appreciate everything I encounter in life."

Now, there will still be unknowns. Like the farmer, you can't predict exactly what will happen to your crop every year. Sometimes the unpredictability of weather and other conditions will change the time of harvest. Something in the environment may even destroy the crop.

But still you learn that if you keep preparing the soil, planting, nurturing, and doing all you can to be a wise steward, over time you will reap what you sow. Though the individual events can't always be predicted, the pattern can be anticipated. If you think in terms of principles, are true to principles, and exercise faith in the results, they will eventually come to pass.

Consider other changeless natural laws and how they affect our roles in life.

- Interdependence: In nature, everything is related to everything else. Consider the complex interrelationship of the food chain, the microorganisms in the soil that allow plants to live, the effect of photosynthesis—of light transforming plant chlorophyll into sugar, creating food for other living things. The problem for us as individuals comes when we look at our lives in terms of mechanical, isolated parts instead of as an organic, highly interrelated whole. Interdependence also helps us to realize that every individual is important, and that each contributes to the welfare of all.

- Growth: Nature teaches that all living things require constant nourishment and nurturing of the conditions that encourage growth. The problem comes when we forget that our own growth requires exercise and nourishment for body, mind, and spirit; when we fail to nurture the relationships and conditions that create growth; when we treat others and organizations as non-living things.

- Order: Nature teaches that some things must come before other things. The planting of the seed and nurturing of the young plant come before the harvest of the mature plant. Aspen groves prepare the earth for the pine trees that follow. Trustworthiness precedes trust. We can't expect to have effective communication until we create the systems and relationships that will produce it.

- Seasons: In nature, there are seasons. There are times of preparing and planting, times of watering and nurturing, times—often intense times—of harvest. Although some are seasons of imbalance, each season contributes to the balance of the whole. Our lives, our families, our communities, and our organizations also have seasons. A new baby, a new business, or a new challenge may create seasons of imbalance. But effectively handled, even these seasons of imbalance help to create the balance of the whole.

- Opposition: Nature teaches the value of opposition and challenge. The turbulent stream purifies the water. By pushing against its cocoon, the butterfly gains sufficient strength to fly. In our own lives and organizations, exercising our muscles—physical, mental, or moral—gives us strength and prevents atrophy. We learn from challenges, failures, and problems to improve life.

- Balance: Nature teaches that balance is a dynamic equilibrium, a synergistic ecosystem in which all parts contribute to the effectiveness of the whole. The problem is when we see balance in a mechanical rather than a natural way. Balance does not require sameness or equality; it requires wholeness and harmony. Diversity and interdependence make a true dynamic equilibrium possible.

Now, this is by no means a complete or comprehensive list of the many principles nature teaches, nor is it intended to be. The point is that these natural laws do exist, and the number of applications for each is endless in our quest for abundance. To understand this is to open the door to a whole new way of seeing, learning, and living. And to live with integrity to these principles provides a powerful source of inner peace and strength—a feeling of abundance.

Choice

> "EVERY OPPORTUNITY PRESENTS A CHOICE. SOME THINGS ARRIVE IN THEIR OWN MYSTERIOUS HOUR, ON THEIR OWN TERMS AND NOT YOURS, TO BE SEIZED OR RELINQUISHED FOREVER."
>
> ~ GAIL GODWIN

Choice is the ultimate principle of human capacity from which all others are derived. Choice empowers us to deal effectively with change and changelessness.

Though human beings are not the only entities in nature that have choice, it is clear that at least two things about human choice are unique:

- The first is that humans have the widest scope of choice. At the same time, they are capable of the most degrading and the most beautiful and uplifting acts in all of nature.

- The second is that humans have moral choice. The scope and nature of human choice is what gives us the responsibility of respectful stewardship with regard to the rest of creation.

Every day we make choices that affect the direction of our lives, our families, our businesses, and our communities. When choices are made with little or no understanding of natural law, they tend to be simplistic, reactionary, myopic, or egotistical. The cost is extreme. At the core, almost every personal, life, business, or historical failure can be traced to poor decision-making.

But when we learn to make choices based on natural principles—to handle change and create change based on changeless laws—we create positive results. Then our choices reflect wisdom and lead to contribution. We recognize that others, too, have choice.

For a life of abundance, choice is where the rubber meets the road. To master the art of living, learn to choose well.

So how can we learn to make better choices? We can choose to look beneath the thin veneer of social conditioning and deep into the true nature of life. We can look for principles, understand and apply them, and live in harmony with them. The more our values are in harmony with those principles, the better decisions we will make...and the more inner peace and abundance we will have.

We are raised to believe that there are single right answers. In hundreds of multiple-choice tests in school, when you give the right answer, you get an "A" grade; give the wrong answer and you flunk. But nature doesn't see it that way. Nature finds thousands of solutions—thousands of "right answers"—to the challenges it faces.

I remember one day when I was on a trek in the Olympic Mountains in Washington State. I looked out into a meadow of flowers, a thousand fantastic shapes and colors all designed for one purpose: to propagate the seed of the mother plant. Nature was saying, "There's more than one right answer!"

We can work to gain a more accurate perspective. We can choose to value interdependence, to believe that there is more than one "right" answer, and to value the diversity that creates synergy.

Embracing Nature

When I began to embrace what nature seemed to be teaching, both my perspective and my actions began to change. I no longer stopped at the first right answer. And when I pressed on, looking for that next right answer, I did so not in fear, but comforted in knowing that it would be there for me. Slowly, I began to embrace change rather than fear it.

Once you discover that there is more than one "right answer" in life, you begin to celebrate the things that lead to multiple right answers, such as the diversity of your life or the concept of empowerment. You realize that good ideas can come from anywhere, and that everyone has something to contribute based on his or her own point of view.

We can choose to nurture our relationship with nature, including our relationships with other people. We can be good stewards of the earth. We can realize that the way we treat nature—particularly animals—is often one of the best mirrors of our relationships with others, as well as a mirror of our own souls. If our paradigm in nature is one of command and control, our paradigm in life is likely the same. And, although we cannot choose what happens to us, we can choose our response to what happens to us.

In making these kinds of choices, we live and lead others based on the natural laws of effectiveness that govern in all of life. And making those positive choices is the difference between being a leader or a victim, abundance or scarcity.

The result, as we open to nature, people, and principles, is that we find the Sky Ridge Promise fulfilled. We get what we need—personally, individually, specifically—for the art of living.

> "IT WAS NOT LIKE TAKING THE VEIL, NO SOLEMN ABJURATION OF THE WORLD, I ONLY WENT OUT FOR A WALK AND FINALLY CONCLUDED TO STAY TILL SUNDOWN FOR GOING OUT I FOUND THAT I WAS REALLY GOING IN." ~ JOHN MUIR

Nature of Gratitude

Perhaps the greatest lesson we can learn from nature is gratitude for the abundance of beauty that surrounds us. As I reflect on my life, I realize how fortunate I have been growing up and living in the Pacific Northwest, and in the mountains around the San Francisco Bay Area. Nature has presented me with an abundance of beauty beyond my wildest imaginings. Over and over again, she seems to be saying, "Relax. There is more here than you will ever need. When you believe it, you will see it."

The more I believe it, the more I do see it…not just in nature, but in my family, in my profession, and in myself. I am filled with gratitude—and happiness. After all, the factor that most determines our happiness is gratitude.

Gratitude…how many times have I, as an amateur photographer, clicked off a shot of a dew drop, or a sunset, or an animal, and as I lower my camera found myself silently murmuring, "Thank you!" Those flashes of gratitude help illuminate the rest of my life. Glancing at a field as I drive down the freeway, I feel a smile pull at my lips as my mind's eye delights in the thousands of breathtaking photos I know are hidden there. So I can't stop to take them all—the fact that I know they're there makes that field a little more special.

Each time nature helps me get in touch with the extraordinariness of this world, my gratitude—my happiness—increases. If we could publish gratitude in our lives everyday, the way nature publishes beauty in every sunrise and every sunset, how different might the world be?

I spent several years on Sky Ridge Ranch, and it was a wonderful time in my life. But then, after all that time living and learning in nature, I thought, "Okay, now how does this apply?" Seeing principles is easy when you're in nature. With the stars, the sky, the oceans, and streams, it's hard to miss seeing them. But it's more of a challenge to integrate it in the world of human beings, where people problems confound you and natural principles are not as easy to see.

As I conclude this chapter, I encourage you to claim the Sky Ridge Promise for yourself. Make the proactive choice to create a deep and meaningful relationship with nature, people, and principles. When you feel challenged or you begin to feel overwhelmed, discouraged, anxious, road-blocked, or out of balance in any arena of life, reconnect with the ever-present reminders of change, changelessness, and choice that are all around you. Be truly open. Seek wisdom. Ask the hard questions. Ponder deeply.

The answers will come. And in carrying them out, you will become a more abundant person in all arenas of your life. That's the nature of abundance and the art of living— the Sky Ridge Promise.

About
Schuyler Morgan

Schuyler Morgan, Professional Certified Coach, is the Founder and President of Catalytic Business Coaching, a combined network of coaches and consultants who offer an array of services to industries worldwide, spanning all aspects of Enterprise Risk for Business Continuity and Crisis Management. Schuyler's reputation precedes her, because of her remarkable skill with leading high impact teams, using the coach approach for peak performance. Since 9/11, she has developed a high impact Executive and Team Crisis Leadership model to fill the missing link in contemporary organizational development for today's complex eWorld, and for leading under fire.

Ms. Morgan delivers her revolutionary eCulture Leadership coaching to individuals, entrepreneurs, teams, and organizations' top talent. She coaches them to radically shift their thinking and break out of their comfort zones, an absolute requirement for a competitive edge in this turbulent age of paradox. Her alertness to cutting edge issues and trends keeps her coaching sharp and focused.

She recently Co-founded Finishing Up – A Contemporary Finishing School with Personal Coaching for Professionals. For anyone who wants to realize their potential and avoid the pitfalls of our eCulture Age of Paradox, this trailblazing venture reminds us that character issues get people hired as well as fired. The absence of strong character may cause damage to teams, to quality, to reputations and the enterprise at large. The advantages of contemporary individual leadership, manners, and etiquette are that they serve as a guide to confidence, enjoyment, civility, and dignity for profiting in the age we live.

Schuyler, a sought-after professional speaker, is often seen as a formidable wit and an irresistible combination of iconoclasm and convention. She doesn't give you rules; she gives you perspective. For those who have stumbled through life wondering if there are any easy answers, the happy news is, Schuyler helps you find them.

She has authored the booklet *The Art of Recognition*, is a contributing author of the book *A Guide to Getting It: Self-Esteem*, and is busy working on her book *Too Busy to Love, Too Tired to Care: Juggling Work and Life in Uncertain and Unreasonable Times*. She also has numerous articles appearing in publications in the U.S. and Canada. She is an alumna of Leadership America, and Editor-in-Chief of the International Coach Federation's Organizational Coach eJournal.

Ms. Morgan is in a unique position to coach individuals and organizations toward their potential by combining her knowledge of human dynamics and high performance organizational cultures. She seems particularly able to understand people and the human factor in situations, especially in today's demanding fast-paced environments. Schuyler has the energy, confidence, and spirit to initiate in all environments, and to influence outcomes, a necessary sign of authentic leadership abilities. These abilities are well developed in her coaching approach. She blends the strength of maturity with the enthusiasm, vigor and spontaneity of youth.

Ms. Morgan resides in Oakland, California. To contact her, phone: 510-653-6868 or email her at Schuyler@eCultureCoach.com. Please visit: www.CatalyticBizCoaching.com , www.eCultureCoach.com and www.FinishingUp.com.

I Believe I Can Fly

By Marilyn French Hubbard

Abundance is that wonderful experience of living a rich and prosperous life. For some, the idea of abundance includes material wealth. For others, abundance is the occurrence of incredible opportunities that are sometimes viewed as serendipitous moments. Our world is full of people experiencing freedom, wealth, and power by being, doing, and having it all, while others are experiencing scarcity, bondage, and unhappily struggling with issues, circumstances, and situations they believe they have no ability to control. Why is it that living an abundant life seems so natural to some and so alien to others?

An analytical friend of mine always marvels about all the wonderful things that seem to happen effortlessly in my life. He always says in amazement, "This is just not logical." My response is, "You're right, it's not logical, it's spiritual." Experiencing abundance begins with your inner, spiritual self, which acts as an intuitive guide for the free flow of abundance. Spiritual growth is similar to personal growth, with one big difference: personal growth is your capacity to stand apart from yourself and examine your thinking, your motives, your history, your scripts, your actions, and your habits and tendencies. When you grow spiritually, you are connecting with a source of a higher power, and using that connection to develop self-confidence, self-love, clarity, and other important qualities to enhance your growth and abundance. When you integrate your personal growth (what you believe about your self), and your spiritual growth (your purpose or spiritual path), the level of abundance is powerfully impacted.

At the heart of any spiritual discipline is the desire to connect with a higher source or center. The source of abundance is that center. The level of internal connection with your spiritual source or center influences your external actions and behaviors.

Whatever your spiritual center is, it is the foundation and source of your security, guidance, wisdom, and power. These represent the following:

- Security: your sense of worth, identity, and self-esteem.

- Guidance: your source of direction or internal frame of reference that governs your moment-to-moment thoughts and actions.

- Wisdom: your perspective on life, your sense of balance and integrated wholeness.

- Power: the strength and energy to make consistent choices and decisions in alignment with your source or center.

Integrating all of these creates a sense of meaning, purpose, congruence, and contribution, allowing you to live for a purpose higher than yourself that inspires and energizes you.

What is Abundance?

Abundance may be defined as prosperity, blessings, wealth, riches, peace, fame, fortune, influence, and affluence. However, don't confuse having money with having abundance. Money can be an outcome of abundance, but the accumulation of money alone is not abundance. Having abundance is a matter of choice. Being abundant requires that you know what you want, what you stand for, and that you live in such a way that what you do and who you are creates an overflowing of goodness. Continual nourishment and renewal of your mind, body, and spirit produces this continuous abundant flow.

Having a sense of abundance helps to turn the impossible into the possible, the mediocre to the incredible, and merely existing to really living. It is giving birth to what can be, rather than what is. Abundance comes when you are ready for it in the proportions that you are prepared to give and receive at any give time.

Many of my coaching assignments have been in support of others as they work to create and sustain rich and prosperous lives. As I work with clients, I hear them asking for abundance in ways that say they aren't yet prepared to make the choices that will bring prosperity into their lives. For example, they ask for:

- A better career opportunity, when they are not giving their current employer an honest day's work.
- More money, when they are not managing the money they already have.
- A new house, when they are not taking care of the home they live in.
- An intimate relationship with another person, when they are not taking care of themselves.

When they observe the abundance others are receiving, they often become disgruntled and discount the steps others took to get the abundance. I sometimes wonder why some individuals don't realize they are their own worst enemy. They desire abundance and feel entitled to it. But, they have dreams they never pursue. They are unwilling to commit to doing the extra work required to gain the blessing of abundance. In the process, they become victims or hurt people. When people are hurt, they tend to hurt other people, adding another layer to block the steady flow of abundance into their lives.

Do you want to have it all? Would you like for money not to be an issue in your life? Would you like to make your dreams come true? Are you doing what you love for a living? Would you like to laugh more often? Would you like to radiate self-esteem, inner peace, love, well-being, and happiness? If you answered yes to these questions, you want to live an abundant life. The next question is, are you ready to do what it takes to start the flow of abundance into your life?

How do You "Get" Abundance?

Butterflies are one of the most beautiful of all insects. Their color, ease, and grace have inspired artists and poets charmed by their delicate, gorgeously colored wings. However, the caterpillar does not start out flying high and knowing what a beautiful butterfly it will become. It starts out low to the ground and spends time in its cocoon.

Creating abundance is like the process of a caterpillar turning into a butterfly. Like an individual, the caterpillar has to have done all of the necessary preparation, to go through various stages of development, change, transformation, and eventually metamorphosis before it can spread its beautiful, abundant wings and travel great distances.

You may be a caterpillar that is ready to be a butterfly. You want to rise above the condition of your current self and become a renewed, abundant self. You want to fly.

The cocoon, an embryonic space for transformation for the caterpillar, and a symbol for a safe haven in which to build strength in your life, is necessary for evolution and transformation. Your cocoon is at once a resting place, and at the same time, a place to grow—the place you are in before an abundant spiritual breakthrough. Like a caterpillar evolving in its cocoon, to become abundant, it is important to spend time in the inner chambers of your life, in solitude, and in a meditative and prayerful state. Your private moments influence your public actions. While you are in your cocoon, you can develop, strengthen, and grow in areas where you are weak and lacking. The more you focus on what you are becoming, the stronger your wings will be when you are ready to soar. When you emerge from your cocoon, you will be a new person. You will have a new conversation and a new kind of thinking. This new abundant way of thinking will enable you to give up the lower caterpillar way of being so you can achieve the higher, butterfly status.

While the process is rewarding, transformation takes diligence and persistence. You achieve abundance by becoming a full butterfly in all areas of your life by balancing yourself mentally, physically, and spiritually. While you are in the process of becoming a butterfly in one area of your life, you may have already become a butterfly in another area of your life. We are all at different stages of abundance and we all have different assignments. When you soar, you tend to find other butterflies. Along the way, you may find caterpillars that are in the process of becoming butterflies, too. In those areas where you are a caterpillar, the other person may have already become a butterfly. That's how we learn from each other and create abundance together.

A butterfly begins its life as a tiny egg, which hatches into a caterpillar. The caterpillar spends most of its time eating and growing, as if sensing the need to prepare for something more in its life.

The first and most important step you can take in bringing abundance into your life is taking the time to expand your vision of yourself and your life. The desire for abundance begins with a tiny seed of thought, a discovery, or a feeling that it is time to grow. You begin to envision your abundant life. This vision will serve like a compass to inspire and energize you.

Expanding your vision is the step that is most likely to be skipped or rushed through because of your need to reach the destination before traveling the journey. When you expand your vision, you can best support yourself by staying focused on this step for as long as it takes to acquire a sense of the breadth and depth of the possibility for your life and the part you play in making your vision a reality. Accepting and having a limited vision for yourself blocks the flow of the endless possibilities that are available to you.

Use your imagination to conjure the images of abundance in all areas of your life. Daydream, be creative, fantasize, discover, and uncover what you want your life to be like. Use your intuition and pay attention to that gut-level feeling that you may not consider logical, explainable, or practical. Look at the big picture of your life. Consider the unlimited potential and magnificence of what is available to you. Consider this intangible part of your life just as valuable as the tangible goals you have set for yourself.

Your dreams have to be nurtured and cultivated to create the abundance you desire. Dedicating the care, emphasis, and time necessary to reflect on and clarify your purpose, passion, missions, assignments, and values contributes to your evolvement. "Think and grow rich" and "first things first" are phrases we often hear regarding this process.

While living in the present moment, seeing beyond your current situation, knowing you have the right to abundance, and getting in touch with what matters to you most, consider questions such as these:

- What is most important to me?
- What do I plan my life around?
- Do I have one center or several?
- What do I feel are my greatest strengths?
- What strengths have others who know me well noticed in me?
- What do I deeply enjoy doing?
- What have been my happiest moments in life?
- Why were they happy?
- When I daydream, what do I see myself doing?
- What talents do I have that no one else knows about?

The caterpillar's skin does not grow in size, and so the caterpillar sheds the old skin and grows a new one. This process is repeated several times. After the caterpillar reaches its full size, it forms a protective shell.

Abundance is a human transformation from the old to the new. Shedding the old and accepting the new requires digging deeper and deeper; identifying the issues, circumstances, misfortunes, situations, and relationships that may be blocking your abundance.

If abundance is missing, something needs to be healed. What is it that is blocking your abundant flow? Anger, depression, resentment, and jealously must be resolved, because those emotions can block the flow of your gifts. What do you need to do to keep the blessings flowing? Keep a clear conscience. Be loyal to your own integrity. You bring into your life what you do in the closets of your mind. As an evolving butterfly, you have to acknowledge the depth of yourself that is trying to emerge.

As you look at ways in which you are growing, ask yourself if you are living up to the calling of your life? Have you discovered your gifts and talents? Are you using those gifts and talents? Discovering, developing, embracing, enjoying, and using your gifts will assure you that you will be abundantly blessed. You might be asking yourself, "If I have a gift, why don't I know it?" You were never taught it. Gifts and talents are something you discover and then develop. They need continued spiritual subsistence in order to grow —just like a baby has to be fed. You may have bondage that hinders the flow of your gifts, like fear that prevents you from developing your full potential. Perhaps you have been trying to be someone other than yourself, have a poor self image, or have not taken responsibility for yourself, which all impede the flow to the natural expression of your abundant gifts and talents.

Your gift is the thing you do well because it is second nature to you. Others notice and celebrate what you do, even though it may seem like nothing to you. That's your gift. Your gift, when set before those who need what you have to offer, opens the door to favors and blessings. Be still long enough to complete what you are called to do.

When you're using gifts, you are investing in your abundance. Gifts and talents are not to be used for selfish purposes. Use your giftedness to abundantly bless others. Your giftedness was not an afterthought. It was part of God's plan to shape you for your role in the universe. Find out what you really love and build your life around it. Understand the importance of your uniqueness. Whatever you are gifted to do is what you should be doing abundantly.

Maintain a giving attitude, and you will know that you have everything to gain. Since you've developed a lasting sense of abundance, you can be truly charitable. You will become preoccupied with prosperity rather than scarcity. Give from the gifts and talents that you abundantly possess and see the abundance in everyone else. Everyone has a gift; no one has been left out. The gifts of others are to be honored and not envied.

Inside the shell, an amazing change occurs – the worm-like caterpillar becomes a beautiful butterfly.

Living in the world as a new, beautiful butterfly instead of a caterpillar, you learn how to speak a new conversation, you have a new way of thinking and behaving. The Bible says, "We are transformed by the renewing of our minds." As our minds and habits change, so does our harvest. A butterfly cannot look forward and backward at the same time, so you look ahead.

Communicate your uniqueness and what you stand for by creating and living by a personal mission statement, philosophy, creed, or personal constitution. Your mission statement is the foundation for your changeless core or compass. Once you have your sense of mission, you have the essence of your direction for finding abundance. However, be open to accepting your abundance in different ways, shapes, and forms that it comes in. Once you are clear on the essence of what you want, you will learn to recognize it when it comes. Ask yourself the following questions:

- Am I being open to having the best thing come?
- Are there other forms that will fulfill the same function in even better ways?
- Can I have the essence of the abundance that I want right now?

When the shell breaks open, the adult butterfly emerges.

Understanding and embracing the notion of abundance attracts abundance. Becoming deeply absorbed in this kind of profound self-knowledge and not emerging unchanged is impossible. You will see the world, relationships, and yourself differently.

The life of an adult butterfly centers on reproduction. The reproduction cycle begins with courtship, in which the butterfly seeks a mate. They look for signals or cues of a certain kind or in a particular order. If the courtship proves successful, mating occurs. If a butterfly presents the wrong cue, or a series of cues in the wrong sequence, it will be rejected. Usually, a butterfly that presents an appropriate scent will be immediately accepted as a mate.

You are prepared to receive your abundance through people, places, and things. Go where you are celebrated, instead of where you are tolerated. Become more conscious of where you are and for whom you work. When you are with the right people, the best will come out in you. Creating your own abundant world requires quality relationships with like-minded people, others who are seeking abundant opportunities that are in line with their assignments. Abundance requires that we work together and remain dependent on each other to grasp everything that is available to us. We can all spread our wings together to develop a collective abundant spirit by sharing visions and synergistic agreements. Give to people who will use your resources and gifts to create positive changes in their lives. Give to help people achieve their higher purposes and paths. Look for ways to make another person a winner. As you help others win, you win as well. Remember, the best gift to give others is the example of your own life working abundantly.

Your individual gift gives only one perspective of the whole. Remember the six blind men who went to "see" an elephant? Six men observed the same thing, but "saw" six different things. The first one felt the side and said an elephant is like a wall; the second one felt the tusk and claimed an elephant is like a spear; the third one felt the trunk and likened it to a snake; the fourth one felt the leg and said the elephant is a tree; the fifth one touched the ear and declared the elephant was like a fan; the sixth one felt the tail and insisted an elephant was like a rope. No one was altogether right, yet no one was entirely wrong. Only when they got all their observations together did they "see" the whole elephant. We live in an interdependent reality of abundance and potential that can only be realized when we interact with others in fully authentic, synergistic ways. How fully developed is the spirit of synergy in your life? Consider using the following affirmations:

- Everything I give to others is a gift to myself.
- As I give I receive.
- Every gift I give serves and empowers other people.
- My prosperity prospers others.
- Everyone's success contributes to my success.

Butterflies have many enemies, including other insects and birds. To escape their enemies, butterflies have developed various means of self-defense.

There is no need to hide your abundance. Don't deny who you are. Those who attack you do not yet know the potential of their abundance. They attack because they believe they are deprived. Do not share their illusions of scarcity, or you will perceive yourself as lacking, too. Continue to give from your abundance as a demonstration to others that the same is available to them. Make the presence of your abundance known to others by the evidence of abundance in your life. The "Serenity Prayer" contains the wisdom I live by: "God, grant me the serenity to accept the things I cannot change; the courage to change the things I can; and the wisdom to know the difference." Faithfully paying attention to the present moment and being mindful of what is and what you are doing now, is abundance itself.

Many butterflies and caterpillars escape harm because they blend with their surroundings and gain extra protection.

Keep abundance in the form of beauty all around you. Your five senses experience abundance by hearing, seeing, touching, tasting, and smelling. Examples are: the flow of water, the smell of the roses, the beauty of the trees, a sunrise, birds chirping, peacefulness, blossoms, the sunset, the touch of the wind and breeze, the tender touch of love, the velvet touch of silk, a taste of a favorite dish. Your environment is important. You do not have to adjust to space created for others. Change the environment rather than accepting what is given to you. Find out what fits for you. Opening yourself to the present moment places you face to face with the beauty right now.

Butterflies cannot live actively in cold weather. Many species of butterflies survive the winter by migrating to warmer areas, where they spend the winter resting and conserving energy for their return flight in the spring.

Go within and renew from time to time. Renew, recharge, revitalize, and replenish your mind, body, and spirit. Keep a journal. If you're not sure why you still do some things that you know are harmful or self-defeating, analyze it, process it, write it down. Keeping a personal journal empowers you to see and improve, on a day-to-day basis, the way you're developing and using your abundance.

Listen to your inner voice. Being still, reflective, and meditative is a condition you might rarely choose or find, so you must create it. Tap into your own wellspring of wisdom. Take time to be still and listen to that deep inner voice. Then, respond to that voice.

Authenticity means living in such a way that who you are, what you believe, and what you do are all in sync. Learning to be your authentic self is the secret to abundance.

When you know who you truly are, you gain an acceptance, a balance that makes you intuitively know you are on your path to abundance. Trust your self. Enjoy the freedom of being responsible for your self. Every moment is an opportunity to be open, alert, and receptive to the abundance of the present moment. You are no longer a caterpillar. You are a butterfly. Spread your wings and fly!

R. KELLEY SAYS, IN THE LYRICS OF *I BELIEVE I CAN FLY*:

"IF I CAN SEE IT

THEN I CAN DO IT

IF I JUST BELIEVE IT

THERE'S NOTHING TO IT

I BELIEVE I CAN FLY

I BELIEVE I CAN TOUCH THE SKY

I THINK ABOUT IT EVERY NIGHT AND DAY

SPREAD MY WINGS AND FLY AWAY

I BELIEVE I CAN SO

I SEE ME RUNNIN' THROUGH THAT OPEN DOOR

I BELIEVE I CAN FLY

I BELIEVE I CAN FLY

I BELIEVE I CAN FLY...

About
Marilyn French Hubbard

As an author, business coach, speaker, facilitator, and senior-level corporate executive, Marilyn French Hubbard, Ph.D., M.C.C., combines her formal education, business experience, and on-going personal growth with her commitment to support individuals and organizations as they create their desired futures. Marilyn is a pioneer and an authority on entrepreneurial and transformational leadership. She assists individuals with bringing focus into their lives and creating their livelihoods by discovering their God-given gifts and talents. She coaches business leaders to embrace diversity and to nurture the human resources within their organizations. She believes there is a link between health, wealth, and spirituality, and that true leaders serve others.

Marilyn's interest in the economic empowerment of women led her to become the founder of the National Association of Black Women Entrepreneurs, a 5,000 member international network for entrepreneurial and enterprising women. Marilyn has inspired and coached thousands of women pursuing their entrepreneurial dreams. Because of her leadership and advocacy on behalf of women and minorities, she has served as an advisor to Michigan governors and mayors, and to the administrations of Presidents Bill Clinton, George H. Bush, Ronald Reagan, and Jimmy Carter.

In her first business book, *Sisters are Cashing In* (2000, Perigee, ISBN 0-399-52572-6), Marilyn integrates business and spiritual principles and offers insights into the emotional, mental, and spiritual factors that can lead you into debt and poverty. She also presents strategies to break negative patterns and help you discover the kind of freedom, wealth, and power that come from having your life in order, doing what you love for a living, and making a contribution to the success of others. Marilyn is also a contributing author of *A Guide to Getting It: Self-Esteem.*

Marilyn is on the senior leadership team and is the Corporate Vice President for Organization and Community Partnerships with the Henry Ford Health System in Detroit, Michigan. She is accountable for aligning the System's mission, vision, and values with its commitment to corporate responsibility by partnering with Human Resources, Government, and Public Affairs in maintaining a corporate culture that supports the health and well being of their 17,000 employees. She also works to create external partnerships that are economically, socially, and environmentally healthy for the community.

Marilyn is a graduate of Ferris State University, The University of Detroit-Mercy, Central Michigan University, and the American Institute. She is certified as a Master Certified Coach by the International Coach Federation.

To contact Marilyn, send an email to MFHubbard@aol.com, or visit the National Association of Black Women Entrepreneurs, Inc. website at www.NABWE.com.